BARTER, MONEY, AND MARKET MECHANICS

How Human Exchange Evolved from Reciprocity to Modern Markets

Rupen O. Adhikari

Published by Quill to Kindle Publishers

First Edition, 2026

To everyone who has ever wondered:

Why do we accept a piece of paper, a number on a screen, or a promise as valuable?

And to everyone who understands that behind every price is a human agreement about value.

"The history of exchange is not simply the history of things changing hands. It is the history of human beings learning how to trust, measure, record, and settle value."

— Rupen O. Adhikari

Table of Contents

PROLOGUE

Before Money, There Was a Problem

Imagine a world without a price tag.

No dollar sign.

No bank account.

No credit card.

No electronic payment.

No cashier waiting to scan a barcode.

You possess something valuable. Perhaps grain. Perhaps fish. Perhaps a tool. Perhaps your labor.

You need something else.

The problem appears simple:

How do you get it?

You might offer what you have to someone who possesses what you need.

But immediately another problem appears.

What if that person does not want what you have?

You have grain.

The carpenter has tools.

But the carpenter already has enough grain.

You need the tools today.

The carpenter needs medical care.

The physician needs shoes.

The shoemaker needs grain.

Suddenly, the problem is no longer simply exchange.

It is **coordination**.

This is the fundamental problem behind the story of barter.

The familiar economic narrative says that humans began with barter, discovered its inconvenience, and eventually created money.

There is truth in that model.

But the complete story is more complicated.

A direct exchange can fail because wants do not match. It can fail because timing does not match. It can fail because quantities do not match. It can fail because neither party trusts the other.

And people have developed many ways to solve those problems.

They created obligations.

They remembered debts.

They gave gifts.

They redistributed resources.

They established units of account.

They developed institutions.

They created commodities that others would accept.

Eventually, different forms of money emerged and became embedded in increasingly complex systems of exchange.

The important lesson is therefore not simply that **money replaced barter**.

The deeper lesson is this:

Human beings repeatedly invent mechanisms that make value transferable across differences in desire, time, distance, trust, and circumstance.

That idea changes how we understand money.

Money is not merely a thing.

It is a mechanism.

A currency note is useful because someone else is willing to accept it.

A bank balance is useful because a system recognizes the claim.

A credit instrument is useful because someone believes the obligation will be honored.

An asset is valuable because people believe it can produce utility, income, scarcity, status, security, or future purchasing power.

Even barter depends on a similar principle.

The item must be useful to someone else.

The agreement must be trusted.

The value must be understood.

The exchange must be completed.

The manuscript that follows begins with barter, but it does not end there.

It moves through credit, debt, reciprocity, gift exchange, silent trade, proto-money, currencies, constrained markets, countertrade, time banks, and alternative exchange systems.

The purpose is not to present one perfectly linear story.

Economic history rarely behaves that way.

Instead, this book asks a more useful question:

What problem is each exchange system trying to solve?

That question allows us to see something surprisingly modern inside ancient economic behavior.

The merchant who accepts a commodity because others will accept it later is thinking about liquidity.

The farmer who extends grain until harvest is thinking about credit.

The community that records obligations is thinking about accounting.

The trader who chooses a neutral exchange point is thinking about transaction risk.

The company that accepts goods instead of cash is thinking about liquidity and settlement.

The person who earns a time credit is participating in a local exchange network.

Different eras.

Different institutions.

Different technologies.

But remarkably similar problems.

The mechanics of markets are ultimately mechanics of human cooperation under conditions of uncertainty.

And once we understand that, we can begin to understand money itself.

CHAPTER 1

Barter vs Money: The Real Distinction

Why Barter Still Matters After Money

What do you actually trade when you exchange a consulting hour for a website redesign, a repair for a favor, or inventory for advertising space? If the answer is simply "something before money," you miss the more useful point: barter remains a distinct trade mode because it solves problems that priced transactions do not always solve well.

Barter removes money from the middle of an exchange. That can preserve cash, move idle capacity, open access to a supplier, or test whether two parties value each other's work. It can also create serious confusion when people treat a barter deal as informal, free, or automatically fair. A cash price gives both sides a common measuring stick. Barter requires them to establish that measure themselves.

Economic history supports this distinction. The familiar textbook sequence says that societies began with barter and later invented money because direct exchange suffered from the "double coincidence of wants": each party had to want what the other offered at the same time and in the right amount. That problem exists, but historians and anthropologists have found little evidence that entire communities organized themselves around pure barter economies. Credit, delayed repayment, gifts, shared stores, taxes, and redistribution often carried more of the daily exchange.

Barter appeared repeatedly at the edges of those systems: between strangers, across communities, during shortages, and after monetary systems weakened. That pattern gives you a practical lesson. Do not ask whether barter represents an earlier stage of money. Ask what function the trade performs now. After reading this section, you can identify that function, price the exchange, record it, and decide when barter strengthens your finances rather than merely disguising a weak deal.

The Trade-Mode Map

The **Trade-Mode Map** classifies an exchange by what carries value through the transaction. It prevents a common error: treating every non-cash arrangement as the same. A gift, a credit agreement, a swap, and a money purchase create different obligations and different risks.

Use the map by checking four questions:

1. **What moves immediately?** Barter involves direct delivery of goods or services in return for goods or services. If one party delivers today and expects payment later, the exchange includes credit. If one party gives without a defined return, it functions more like a gift or favor.

2. **What sets the value?** A money transaction uses a quoted price. A barter transaction needs a reference price, such as a normal hourly rate, retail price, wholesale invoice, or recent comparable sale. Without that reference, both parties may confuse enthusiasm with value.

3. **When does each obligation end?** A clean barter ends when both sides deliver the agreed items or services. A continuing obligation creates a running account, membership arrangement, or informal

credit system. Write down the end point because vague future favors create disputes.

4. **What happens if one side fails?** Money provides a clear remedy: refund, replacement, or collection. Barter requires a specific substitute. Decide whether the defaulting party owes cash, equivalent services, a replacement item, or nothing because the other party accepted the risk.

Consider three examples. A plumber repairs a gym's leaking shower in exchange for six months of membership. That is barter if both parties define the repair and membership clearly. A consultant completes work now in exchange for a promise of introductions later. That is not simple barter; the return remains uncertain, so the consultant carries credit risk. A neighbor gives a designer an old laptop with no agreed return. That is a gift, even if the designer later helps with a logo.

Leila, a 34-year-old freelance consultant, can apply the map before accepting a proposed exchange. Her normal project rate is $150 per hour. A local studio offers four hours of studio access, valued at $400, for a two-hour customer-research session. The deal looks attractive only after Leila checks the conditions: whether she can use the hours during valuable times, whether the studio has suitable equipment, whether the access expires, and whether she would otherwise pay $400 for it. The map turns "That sounds useful" into a measurable decision.

A practical barter agreement should state:

- each party's exact deliverable; - the agreed reference value; - the delivery date or usable period; - quality standards and limits; - cancellation and replacement terms; - tax and recordkeeping responsibilities.

The agreement does not make barter less personal. It protects the relationship by removing avoidable uncertainty.

Putting the Trade-Mode Map Into Practice

Leila receives a proposal from a web designer: she will provide six hours of customer interviews and analysis, and the designer will rebuild her consulting website. Leila normally charges $150 per hour, so her contribution has a reference value of $900. The designer quotes the website at $1,200 for a cash client, but the quote includes three pages, mobile formatting, basic search settings, and one revision round.

Leila should not accept the $1,200 figure automatically. She needs to compare both sides under the same conditions.

1. **Define the deliverables.** Leila writes "six one-hour interviews, interview guide, transcript summary, and a two-page findings memo." The designer writes "three-page website, mobile layout, contact form, basic search settings, and one revision round." This prevents a broad promise such as "customer research for a new site."

2. **Set reference values.** Leila values her work at $900. She checks whether the designer's $1,200 quote reflects the actual scope and whether another provider would charge $900 to $1,000 for the same work. If the site normally sells for $1,200 but the designer expects only a light template change, the quoted value may overstate the return.

3. **Compare usefulness, not labels.** Leila estimates that a finished site would replace a $300 cash landing-page purchase and save roughly ten hours of setup work. She assigns the site a practical value of $1,000, not because the designer wrote $1,200 on the proposal, but because that amount matches her realistic alternative.

4. **Resolve the imbalance.** Leila's $900 contribution falls $100 below the site's practical value. They agree that she will add a one-hour follow-up call, while the designer will include a second revision round. The revised exchange gives both sides a clear reason to proceed.

5. **Control timing.** Leila schedules the interviews for Monday and Tuesday. The designer delivers the first website draft within seven days of receiving the findings memo. Neither side must wait indefinitely for the other.

6. **Record the transaction.** Each party records the normal value of the goods or services, the date, and any applicable tax information. Barter can create taxable income even when no cash changes hands, so Leila asks her accountant how to report the exchange in her jurisdiction.

The expected outcome is not merely a completed website. Leila preserves cash, receives a defined business asset, and avoids giving away six hours for an uncertain promise. The designer receives research that improves the site and avoids spending cash on an outside researcher. Both parties gain because the exchange uses idle or complementary capacity.

Quick checklist

- Write each deliverable in measurable terms. - Use ordinary cash prices as reference points. - Check whether each item has real use or only advertised value. - Balance differences with a small cash payment or extra deliverable. - Set dates, revision limits, and cancellation terms. - Record the exchange at its agreed market value. - Confirm tax treatment before delivery. - Reassess the deal if either party changes the scope.

The map also helps you reject a poor exchange quickly. If Leila cannot use the studio hours before they expire, the $400 quoted value means little. If the website designer cannot explain what "full redesign" includes, Leila should not trade six billable hours for it. Barter works best when each party holds something valuable to the other and can define that value without pretending that money has disappeared from the calculation.

What to Watch For

Mistaking a promise for a delivered asset

A future introduction, referral, social-media mention, or promise of "more work later" does not equal a completed barter return. It creates uncertainty about timing, quality, and control.

Do this: assign a deadline and a measurable result. If Leila trades two consulting hours for three qualified client introductions, the agreement should define the introduction, the deadline, and what happens if fewer than three arrive.

Not this: accept "I will send business your way" as equal to a $300 service.

Ignoring the cash alternative

A barter offer may look attractive because the stated retail value sounds high. The relevant comparison is what you would actually buy, sell, or save at ordinary market prices.

Do this: record three figures: your normal selling price, the other party's realistic cash price, and your personal use value. Reject the deal when the return has little practical value even if its advertised price looks impressive.

Not this: trade $900 of billable work for $1,200 of equipment that you would not buy for $300.

Treating barter as outside the rules

Barter does not automatically avoid taxes, contracts, licensing requirements, or consumer protections. A service exchange can still involve professional standards, privacy obligations, and taxable income. A product exchange can still involve warranties and defects.

Do this: keep the written agreement, invoice or valuation record, delivery confirmation, and any tax documents. For regulated work, confirm that the exchange complies with the relevant licensing rules.

Not this: rely on a handshake because no cash changed hands.

Barter is neither primitive money nor free trade. It is a recurring market mode that reallocates goods, services, time, and access when direct matching creates a better result than a cash purchase. The Trade-Mode Map gives you a disciplined way to see what the exchange actually does, measure its value, and protect yourself from vague obligations. Once you separate barter from credit, gifts, and money transactions, you can use it deliberately rather than treating it as an informal exception to the market.

CHAPTER 2

The Double-Coincidence Problem

The Big Picture: Why Direct Exchange Breaks Down

A direct exchange can fail in three separate ways: the other party may want something different, need it at another time, or require a different quantity. A retail buyer with 40 cases of surplus stock may find a supplier who wants some of that stock, but not until next quarter, and not in exchange for the exact goods the buyer needs today. The goods have value, yet the trade still cannot happen.

That tension sits at the center of the **Want-Match Friction Model**. Direct exchange requires three matches at once: wants, timing, and quantities. When one match fails, the parties must negotiate, search for another trading partner, accept an uneven deal, or abandon the exchange. Money later reduced this friction by giving each party a transferable claim that did not depend on finding one perfect trading partner.

Darius, a 41-year-old retail buyer, sees this problem in practical terms. His store has 120 insulated water bottles left from a summer promotion. A local gym wants 30 bottles, but it offers personal-training sessions. Darius needs shelving, not training. A shelving supplier might accept bottles, but it wants 200 units and cannot deliver for six weeks. The goods, timing, and quantities refuse to line up.

Key insight: direct exchange does not fail because people lack valuable goods; it fails because value rarely arrives in matching form, at matching times, and in matching amounts.

Key Principles: The Want-Match Friction Model

1. Wants must match in both direction and usefulness.

A trade requires each party to value what the other offers. Darius may value shelving at $1,200 and possess bottles that could sell for $1,200 at retail, but the shelving supplier may have no use for bottles. The supplier may already have full shelves, a different customer base, or a contract that prevents it from accepting merchandise.

This distinction matters because equal market value does not create equal usefulness. A plumber may need a new van, while a vehicle dealer may need electrical work. The plumber's labor can hold substantial value, but the dealer cannot necessarily use it. Direct exchange works only when the offered item solves the other party's current problem.

Before proposing a barter deal, write down both sides:

- What you offer - What the other party actually needs - What you need now - Whether the other party can use your offer without selling it first

If either party must find a third person before receiving value, the original exchange contains hidden friction.

2. Timing can destroy an otherwise fair trade.

Needs have deadlines. A restaurant may need refrigeration repaired before Saturday's service. A contractor may offer future renovation work, but that promise does not help if the restaurant needs a repair today. Likewise, Darius may accept shelving six weeks from now only if his store can safely hold inventory until then.

Timing creates a difference between nominal value and usable value. A $1,000 service next year cannot always replace a $1,000 item needed this week. The delay may force borrowing, lost sales, emergency purchases, or storage costs. Those costs reduce the real value of the proposed exchange.

Record the date each party needs delivery, not merely the estimated price. A trade that looks even on paper may become uneven after adding delay. If Darius loses a display opportunity during a six-week wait, the shelving supplier must offer additional value or a faster delivery to make the exchange workable.

3. Quantities must match closely enough to settle the trade.

Darius has 120 bottles. The gym wants 30. If one bottle carries an agreed trade value of $8, the gym offers $240 of services. That may leave Darius with 90 unwanted bottles and no way to use the remaining value. The exchange solves only part of his inventory problem.

The reverse problem also occurs. A supplier may want 200 bottles, while Darius needs only $1,200 of shelving. If the supplier values each bottle at $8, Darius would need to provide $1,600 of goods. He must either accept extra shelving, add another item, or find a second trade partner.

Quantity mismatch often produces informal debt. One party promises to "make up the difference later," but the promise lacks a clear unit, date, or enforcement method. Record the exact quantity, delivery date, and remaining balance. If the parties cannot state what remains owed, the barter agreement has become an uncertain credit arrangement.

4. Every extra trading partner adds search and settlement risk.

A three-way exchange can solve a want mismatch. Darius could give bottles to the gym, receive training sessions, and transfer those sessions to a store employee who provides shelving installation. But each additional party must agree on value, timing, quality, and delivery. One refusal can stop the chain.

This structure resembles barter only on the surface. It depends on trust, records, and delayed settlement. Money handles the same problem more cleanly because Darius can sell bottles to one buyer and pay the shelving supplier separately. The buyer does not need to want shelving, and the supplier does not need to want bottles.

A Practical Walkthrough: Testing a Barter Deal

Use the Want-Match Friction Model before you accept a direct exchange. The following example uses Darius's 120 surplus bottles and a shelving supplier.

1. **Set a realistic value for the offered goods.** Darius checks recent selling prices rather than relying on the original retail price. The bottles originally sold for $12 each, but the remaining stock moves slowly. He estimates a realistic cash-sale value of $6 per bottle, producing a total value of $720.

2. **Define the exact need.** Darius needs three metal shelving units. The supplier quotes $900, including delivery and assembly. Darius does not treat the $900 quote as automatically equal to $900 of bottles. He asks whether the supplier wants merchandise and, if so, what kind.

3. **Test the want match.** The supplier sells warehouse equipment and does not sell drinkware. It agrees to accept bottles only at $4 each because it would need to resell them. At that rate, Darius must provide 225 bottles to cover $900, but he owns only 120. The want match fails on value and quantity.

4. **Test the timing match.** The supplier can deliver in six weeks. Darius needs the shelving in two weeks for a new product display. The timing match also fails. Even if both parties agreed on value, the delay would leave Darius without the display during the planned sales period.

5. **Calculate the direct-exchange gap.** Darius compares the options:

Option	Immediate result	Main friction
Direct bottle-for-shelving trade	120 bottles at $4 = $480	$420 value gap; six-week delay
Cash sale, then shelving purchase	Sell bottles for about $720; pay $900	Requires $180 cash
Three-way exchange	Bottles to gym; training services to another party	Two extra agreements and uncertain timing

6. **Search for a second party only when the numbers justify it.** A local gym agrees to buy 80 bottles at $6 each, paying with $480 of services. Darius does not need personal training, so he offers the sessions to a nearby business in exchange for $480 of cash or store fixtures. The gym accepts only if Darius delivers all 80 bottles within seven days. The added party creates work, but the terms remain measurable.

7. **Separate the transactions in writing.** Darius records the bottle delivery, the gym's service obligation, the service transfer, and the shelving purchase as separate agreements. Each document states

quantity, value, date, and remedy for non-delivery. He avoids treating a chain of promises as one vague trade.

8. **Compare the result with the cash alternative.** If Darius sells all 120 bottles at $6, he receives $720 and must find the remaining $180 for shelving. If the three-way arrangement converts 80 bottles into $480 and he sells the remaining 40 for $240, he reaches the same $720 total but spends time coordinating services. The barter route makes sense only if the services or fixtures offer more practical value than cash and the delivery risk remains low.

9. **Use a stop rule.** Darius stops negotiating if the arrangement requires more than three parties, more than two weeks of coordination, or an unpriced promise. This rule protects him from spending labor to recover value that he could obtain more simply through a cash sale.

The result does not prove that barter lacks value. It shows where barter works: when both parties want the goods, need them within compatible time frames, and can settle the quantities without creating a long chain of obligations.

Troubleshooting: When the Match Breaks

Problem: Both parties want the exchange, but one party cannot use the offered goods.

Why it happens: Direct value and usable value differ. The shelving supplier may recognize that bottles can sell, but resale requires storage, marketing, and time. The supplier discounts the bottles to account for those costs.

Fix: Ask the recipient to price the goods according to their actual use, then compare that price with a cash sale. If the recipient values the goods below your realistic cash value, do not pretend the values match.

Sell the goods, or find a recipient with a direct use. Darius improved his position when he approached a gym that could give the bottles to members rather than a shelving supplier that would need to resell them.

Problem: The quantities leave a balance that nobody can settle cleanly.

Why it happens: One item often comes in fixed units while the requested service or equipment comes in a different scale. Darius's 120 bottles could not cover a $900 shelving order at the supplier's accepted value of $4 each.

Fix: Divide the exchange into explicit units. Darius could trade 80 bottles for $480 of services, sell 40 bottles for $240, and pay the remaining shelving balance in cash. He should reject phrases such as "we will settle the rest later." State the remaining amount, deadline, and form of payment before delivering anything.

Problem: The trade looks fair, but the delivery dates do not line up.

Why it happens: Parties compare prices while ignoring the cost of waiting. Darius needed shelving in two weeks, while the supplier could deliver in six. The four-week gap threatened the store display and reduced the practical value of the trade.

Fix: Put dates beside every obligation. If one party delivers late, add a specific remedy: a price reduction, replacement service, or cash payment. If the delay creates a business loss that exceeds the benefit of barter, end the negotiation. A trade should reduce friction, not replace a purchase with a project-management burden.

Direct exchange remains useful when the Want-Match Friction Model shows three clean matches: the recipient wants the offered goods, both parties need delivery within compatible periods, and the quantities settle without unresolved balances. When those matches fail, money does more than change the form of payment. It separates the act of selling from the act of buying, allowing each party to find the best counterparty independently. That separation explains why markets can grow beyond small circles of mutual need - and why every exchange system must solve the same basic problem of matching value to action.

CHAPTER 3

Aristotle and Adam Smith's Barter Story

Setting the Stage: What the Classic Story Explains - and Misses

"Money arose because barter was inconvenient." That sentence captures the familiar account associated with Aristotle and Adam Smith. It also hides several separate claims that require testing.

The account begins with direct exchange: a farmer offers grain for tools, while a toolmaker offers tools for grain. Trade works only when both parties want what the other person has, at the same time, in suitable quantities. Money appears as the practical solution. It becomes a medium of exchange, a unit for comparing prices, and a way to hold purchasing power between transactions.

That explanation gets an important point right. Direct barter creates real coordination problems. If a plumber wants a $300 repair from a printer, the printer must want plumbing work worth roughly $300 at that moment. If the printer instead needs accounting help, the plumber must find another exchange partner. Money breaks that chain. It lets the plumber serve one customer, receive payment, and buy from someone else.

The oversimplification comes from treating barter as the universal starting point for organized economic life. Historical evidence also shows credit, gift exchange, debt records, communal redistribution, and delayed reciprocity. Mesopotamian clay tablets recorded rations and obligations long before modern coins circulated widely. Within a settled community, people often tracked who owed what rather than completing an immediate swap.

For a practical analysis, gather three materials: a written description of the exchange, the historical setting, and the actual settlement method. The point is not to choose between "Smith was right" and "Smith was wrong." The point is to identify which part of the classic account fits the evidence and which part turns a useful model into a misleading origin story.

The Smithian Narrative Test: Separate the Useful Mechanism from the Historical Claim

The **Smithian Narrative Test** examines a barter explanation in four passes. It asks whether the exchange involved direct goods or services, whether the parties faced a matching problem, whether another system handled the obligation, and whether money solved the specific problem described.

Begin with the transaction itself. Record what each party supplied, what each party expected, and when settlement occurred. A direct swap requires two linked transfers. A credit arrangement may involve one transfer now and repayment later. A gift exchange may create an obligation without a fixed price or deadline. These forms can exist in the same society, so classify the actual transaction rather than the society as a whole.

Next, test the double coincidence of wants. This means that each party must want the other party's offering in the right amount and at the right time. Suppose a carpenter values 20 bushels of grain at $500, while a farmer needs a $200 repair. The carpenter cannot complete the exchange cleanly unless someone accepts the remaining value or both parties renegotiate. Money removes this exact mismatch by giving both sides a common settlement instrument.

Then ask how the community handled obligations that did not settle immediately. A recorded debt, a promised return favor, shared storage, or a leader's redistribution system can support trade without direct barter. If the evidence shows those mechanisms, the claim "money emerged from barter" becomes too broad. A more accurate statement might read: "Money helped certain exchanges overcome the limits of direct barter, while credit and redistribution handled many other transactions."

Finally, test the causal conclusion. Did the appearance of money follow a demonstrated barter problem, or did authorities introduce a unit for taxes, wages, rations, and accounting? These possibilities can overlap. A market trader may value coins because they ease exchange, while a government may standardize a unit because it simplifies records and collections.

Nora, a 29-year-old history podcaster, can apply the test to a simple case involving a Mesopotamian ration record. Her first draft says, "Workers received goods because barter had failed, so money developed." That draft makes two unsupported jumps. The record may show accounting and distribution, not direct barter. It may also show obligations managed through an institution rather than through private swapping.

She revises the analysis:

| Question | Finding | Result | |---|---|---| | Was the exchange direct? | The record lists rations owed to workers. | Not enough evidence for barter. | | Did both parties need each other's goods immediately? | No matching desire appears. | The double coincidence

problem does not explain the transaction. | | Did an accounting system track value? | Yes, quantities and obligations were recorded. | Credit or redistribution may have organized settlement. | | Did money solve a specific problem? | A standard unit could simplify records and payments. | The claim becomes narrower and stronger. |

The outcome is not a rejection of Smith's insight. Direct exchange really does become difficult as specialization grows. The correction concerns scope. Barter explains one pressure that favors money; it does not automatically explain every early payment, obligation, or economic institution.

Use the same discipline when evaluating modern claims. If a business says it "returned to barter," check whether it actually exchanged services directly or used credits, invoices, trade dollars, or a platform ledger. A $1,000 advertising credit exchanged for $1,000 of repairs may resemble barter, but the credit unit performs some functions associated with money. Labels matter less than the settlement mechanics.

Try It Yourself: Audit a Barter-Origin Claim

Use Nora's podcast research method to examine one claim about barter and money. You need a notebook or spreadsheet, one historical source or business example, and 30 minutes. Choose a claim such as: "People invented money because they could not find someone who wanted their goods."

Write the claim at the top of the page. Under it, create four columns: direct exchange, matching problem, alternative settlement, and money's specific function.

Now fill the columns with concrete evidence. For a modern example, use a local service exchange. Assume a podcast producer offers four hours of editing valued at $400 to a gym owner. The gym owner offers one month of membership valued at $120. The producer does not need a membership, so the direct swap fails. The gym owner then offers two memberships to another editor, who accepts them and edits the podcast. The exchange has now become a chain of obligations rather than a simple two-person barter.

Record the values:

- Editing supplied: $400 - Membership value offered: $120 - Remaining mismatch: $280 - Additional memberships required at $120 each: three, if the editor accepts only memberships - Alternative settlement: a $400 payment or a mixed payment of $120 in membership value plus $280 in money

The expected outcome is a precise diagnosis. The double coincidence problem appears clearly: the first producer does not want the offered service. But the example also shows that barter can continue through intermediaries, credits, or partial payment. Money is not the only possible solution; it is the most flexible settlement tool when participants need different things.

For a historical source, mark every sentence that proves direct exchange and every sentence that merely describes goods, prices, debts, or rations. A list of grain prices does not prove that people swapped grain directly for tools. A debt tablet does not prove that barter preceded the accounting system. Separate observation from interpretation.

Finish by writing a two-sentence conclusion. Sentence one should state what the classic account explains. Sentence two should state what it leaves out. Nora's conclusion might read: "The barter model explains why a common medium helps strangers trade when their wants do not match. The evidence does not establish barter as the organizing system for all earlier economic activity, because credit, redistribution, and recorded obligations also handled exchange."

Completion check:

- You identified a specific direct exchange or confirmed that no direct exchange appears. - You measured the mismatch in goods, timing, or value. - You named at least one alternative settlement system. - You assigned money a specific function rather than treating it as a universal explanation.

Common Pitfalls in Reading the Barter Story

Mistake: Treating a model as a historical record

The classic account works well as a model of why money helps trade. It does not, by itself, prove that every society passed through a pure barter stage. The cause usually lies in confusing a logical sequence with an observed historical sequence.

Do this: Label each statement as either "model," "evidence," or "inference." Use the model to explain the double coincidence problem, then cite the actual record before making a historical claim.

Not this: "Barter was the first economy because economists describe the problem that money solves."

Mistake: Calling every non-monetary exchange barter

A gift, a debt, a ration, and a direct swap do not operate the same way. A gift may create a social obligation without a price. A debt sets a future obligation. A ration distributes goods through an institution. Barter links two immediate offerings.

Do this: Write down whether the exchange settled immediately, created a future obligation, or moved goods through a central storehouse. Apply the label only after checking the settlement process.

Not this: "No coins changed hands, so the transaction was barter."

Mistake: Assuming money solved only one problem

Money can address mismatched wants, but it also supports price comparison, accounting, delayed payment, and saving. Different societies may adopt or standardize money for different reasons. The cause usually lies in forcing one explanation onto several functions.

Do this: Name the exact function involved. If a unit records worker rations, call attention to accounting. If coins allow a trader to sell today and buy later, identify their role as a medium of exchange and store of value.

Not this: "Money appeared for one reason, and every later use follows from that origin."

The strongest conclusion preserves the mechanism without overstating the history: direct barter creates genuine friction, but economies have always used several ways to manage obligations. Understanding that distinction improves how you read monetary history - and how you evaluate modern currencies, credits, and assets that perform money-like functions.

CHAPTER 4

Caroline Humphrey's "Myth of Barter"

What the "Myth of Barter" Actually Claims

A trader leaves a bundle of salt at a neutral meeting place, returns later, and finds grain where the salt stood. No coins change hands. No contract records the exchange. The scene looks like barter, but it tells us almost nothing about whether barter organized the surrounding economy. It may represent a rare trade between strangers, a response to danger, or an exchange used only because the participants lacked a shared currency.

That distinction drives Caroline Humphrey's "Myth of Barter." **Barter** means the direct exchange of goods or services without money serving as the intermediary. **A barter economy** means something stronger: a society in which direct exchange provides the main structure for ordinary economic life. Humphrey's claim was not that people never swapped goods. Her claim was that researchers had not found a society built on pure barter that later invented money through a simple, traceable progression.

The traditional account begins with a village where a farmer wants tools and a toolmaker wants grain. Their problem, called the **double coincidence of wants**, arises because each person must want exactly what the other offers at the same time. Money supposedly solves that problem by giving both parties a common medium. Anthropological evidence complicates this sequence. Many communities handled obligations through credit, gift exchange, shared storage, tribute, redistribution, or delayed repayment long before they used coins. A household could provide food today because the community expected future help, not because it calculated an immediate swap.

The practical consequence matters for anyone studying markets. If barter did not generally precede money, then money did not simply emerge as a clever tool for reducing trading friction. Money also developed from accounting, authority, debt, taxation, ritual obligations, and relationships among groups. The origin of money therefore requires more than asking, "What replaced barter?" It requires asking, "What system already recorded and settled obligations?"

How to Test Whether Barter Organized an Economy

Start by separating an observed exchange from an economic system. A single swap proves only that two parties exchanged goods directly. It does not prove that households used barter for rent, wages, food distribution, taxes, or long-term obligations.

The Evidence Threshold Rule provides a disciplined way to assess historical claims: **do not call a society a barter economy until the evidence shows that barter handled ordinary, repeated, central transactions across the community**. This rule prevents a common mistake. Researchers often find a dramatic exchange between outsiders and then treat it as evidence for the entire society. The exchange may instead reveal the boundary between two economic systems.

Apply the rule in sequence:

1. **Identify the participants.** Determine whether the exchange involved neighbors, relatives, institutions, strangers, or hostile groups.

Direct trade appears more plausible between groups that lack shared obligations, language, or trust. Within a close community, credit and reciprocity often make immediate swapping unnecessary.

2. **Identify the purpose.** Ask whether the exchange supplied daily necessities or served a narrow purpose. A market for foreign metals, ceremonial objects, or luxury goods does not establish a barter system for food and labor.

3. **Check the timing.** Immediate exchange looks different from delayed settlement. If one party gives grain now and receives tools after harvest, the arrangement resembles credit even if no coins appear. The absence of money does not automatically create barter.

4. **Look for records of value.** Clay tokens and cuneiform tablets from ancient Mesopotamia recorded rations, debts, deliveries, and obligations. Such records matter because they show economic calculation without requiring direct swaps. A society may lack coins while still using a unit of account.

5. **Measure reach.** Ask how widely the practice operated. Did barter connect two trading partners, or did it organize household production, wages, public storage, taxation, and redistribution? The second condition demands much stronger evidence.

6. **Compare alternatives.** Examine gift exchange, communal storage, tribute, debt, and redistribution before labeling an exchange barter. A worker who receives food from a communal storehouse has not necessarily traded labor for food at a negotiated rate. The arrangement may reflect membership, rank, duty, or political authority.

This method also clarifies "silent trade," in which parties leave goods at a neutral location without direct contact. Silent trade can reduce the danger of meeting strangers or hostile groups. It demonstrates negotiation under limited trust, not a complete economic order. The participants may still rely on credit, kinship, authority, or established measures within their own communities.

The same caution applies to prehistoric exchange. Informal transfers almost certainly occurred among hunter-gatherers and early agricultural groups. But physical evidence rarely reveals the social meaning of each transfer. A stone tool found far from its source could reflect trade, migration, gift giving, marriage ties, tribute, or movement within a group. The object alone cannot identify the system that moved it.

The Evidence Threshold Rule therefore asks for converging evidence. A strong case needs repeated exchanges, broad participation, clear terms, and proof that direct swaps handled core economic obligations. Without that combination, "barter economy" remains an assumption rather than a conclusion.

Applying the Rule to a Field Investigation

Omar, a 37-year-old field researcher, examines reports of coastal communities that exchanged fish for inland grain. Several accounts describe direct swaps at a seasonal meeting point. One report calls the gathering a barter market and treats it as evidence that money developed later to solve the double coincidence of wants.

Omar does not accept the label immediately. He records each exchange and tests it against the Evidence Threshold Rule.

First, he maps the participants. The fishers and grain producers come from different communities and meet only during a short seasonal window. That fact raises the possibility that direct exchange served as a boundary practice between groups rather than the normal arrangement inside either community.

Next, he examines what happened within each community. The records show households sharing food during shortages, elders allocating stored grain, and families repaying help after harvest rather than at the moment of service. These practices weaken the claim that barter organized daily life.

Omar then checks measurement. Traders used baskets and weights to compare fish and grain, but local administrators also recorded grain obligations separately. The presence of measures and records shows that the communities understood value through more than direct swapping.

Finally, he compares the seasonal exchange with other transactions:

Evidence	What it shows	What it does not show
Fish exchanged directly for grain	Trade occurred between groups	Barter organized the whole economy
Seasonal meeting point	Participants lacked regular contact	Money evolved directly from barter
Shared food during shortages	Communities used social obligations	Every transfer operated as a gift
Records of grain duties	People tracked obligations and quantities	Coins were required for accounting

Omar's conclusion becomes narrower and stronger: the evidence supports limited intercommunity barter, alongside internal sharing, redistribution, and recorded obligations. He rejects the larger claim because the evidence does not show barter handling wages, taxes, household support, or routine exchange within the communities.

That conclusion produces a better practical interpretation. The seasonal market likely existed because the groups had different resources and limited trust. Direct exchange allowed them to settle a transaction without creating a long-term obligation. Inside each community, however, established relationships made delayed repayment and redistribution more efficient than constant one-for-one swaps.

For a modern reader, the same logic helps evaluate claims about informal markets. A local business may trade services with another business during a cash shortage. That transaction proves barter can solve a specific problem. It does not prove that the businesses operate in a barter economy. To make that claim, you would need evidence that barter consistently handles payroll, supplier accounts, taxes, pricing, and customer purchases. Most businesses still use money for those functions, even when they barter occasionally.

Lessons from the Evidence Gap

Takeaway: A direct exchange is evidence of barter, not evidence of a barter economy. Always separate the event from the system. Record who traded, why they traded, how often they traded, and whether the same method handled ordinary obligations. A single exchange between strangers may reveal a special circumstance rather than the society's normal economic structure.

Takeaway: The absence of coins does not mean the absence of money-like functions. A society can track value through grain measures, labor duties, debts, or administrative records without minting coins. When you study an early economy, look for units of account, settlement rules, and records of obligation. These systems may perform essential monetary functions before physical currency appears.

Takeaway: The origin of money likely involved relationships and institutions, not only trading convenience. Credit, redistribution, taxation, authority, and social obligations can explain why people needed ways to measure and settle value. The better question is not simply why people abandoned barter. Ask which existing obligations required durable records, accepted units, and reliable settlement.

The Key actions are straightforward: classify each exchange by participants and purpose; test whether it handled routine community obligations; search for credit, sharing, redistribution, and accounting; and apply the Evidence Threshold Rule before making a broad historical claim. This approach replaces a neat but weak origin story with a more accurate view of how exchange systems develop - and gives you a sharper foundation for understanding money, markets, and asset value.

CHAPTER 5

Credit, Debt, and Reciprocity First

The Foundation: Credit Came Before the Swap

When a community stored grain in a shared granary, a family could draw food before its harvest arrived and repay the obligation later. No one needed to find a farmer who wanted tools at that exact moment. The record of the obligation, the reputation of the household, and the community's expectation of repayment carried the exchange.

That pattern challenges the familiar story that economies moved neatly from barter to money. Barter certainly existed, especially between strangers, distant groups, and communities that lacked trust. Yet many societies organized daily economic life through credit, gift exchange, shared storage, and delayed reciprocity. Mesopotamian clay tablets recorded rations, debts, and deliveries long before minted coins became common. In other settings, households contributed labor or food and received support later, when their circumstances changed.

The **Sequence Reversal Lens** helps you examine an exchange in the correct order. Instead of asking, "What goods can these two people swap right now?" ask three questions: Who trusts whom? What obligation does the exchange create? What system records or enforces repayment? These questions reveal why credit often solved the double coincidence of wants before money solved it through a common medium.

Credit here does not mean a bank loan alone. It means a present transfer supported by a future obligation. A neighbor provides labor today because the recipient will return labor later. A communal store releases grain now because the household will contribute after harvest. A merchant delivers goods before receiving payment because the buyer has an established record. Reciprocity means the exchange moves in both directions, but not necessarily at the same time or in equal form.

That distinction matters for modern wealth building. A business owner who understands delayed reciprocity can separate a useful relationship from an informal arrangement that quietly drains cash. The historical lesson does not say that everyone should lend freely. It says that every credit arrangement needs a clear obligation, a trusted record, and a workable repayment path.

Understanding the Process: Apply the Sequence Reversal Lens

Start with the first stage: identify the relationship. A community member, repeat customer, supplier, or stranger does not carry the same level of credit risk. Historical credit systems depended heavily on repeated interaction and public reputation. A person who expected to meet the same neighbors next week had a reason to honor an obligation. A stranger at a distant trading post had fewer reasons to do so, which made immediate barter or payment more attractive.

Next, identify what moves now and what moves later. Write down the present contribution in plain terms: "four hours of repair work," "two bags of grain," or "$300 of materials delivered today." Then define the future obligation: "four hours of electrical work within 60 days," "replacement grain after harvest," or "payment in two installments." Avoid phrases such as "we will settle up." They leave the value, timing, and responsibility unclear.

The third stage tests whether the community or business can measure the obligation. Ancient accounting systems used tokens and tablets because memory alone could not support a growing network of claims. A modern equivalent might use a dated invoice, shared spreadsheet, receipt, or signed service agreement. The tool matters less than the record. Include the item, quantity, agreed value, due date, and what happens if circumstances change.

The fourth stage separates reciprocity from equality. A reciprocal exchange does not always return the same object or the same amount immediately. A community organizer may receive donated meeting space now and later provide volunteer labor, publicity, or access to a useful network. The arrangement remains sound only when both sides understand the expected return and can decline without punishment.

Finally, review the obligation at a fixed interval. For a short business arrangement, check it weekly until completion. For seasonal support, review it at each agreed milestone, such as planting, harvest, or delivery. If the other party misses a milestone, address the problem immediately. Delay makes a small misunderstanding harder to resolve and turns social trust into unpriced financial exposure.

The Sequence Reversal Lens therefore follows this order:

1. Relationship and trust. 2. Present contribution. 3. Future obligation. 4. Record and enforcement. 5. Review and settlement.

This sequence differs from a simple barter search. Barter asks whether two parties possess matching wants now. Credit-first analysis asks whether the parties can support a reliable promise across time.

Applying the Knowledge: Priya's Community Exchange Ledger

Priya, 32, organizes a neighborhood food program. Local growers can provide vegetables after harvest, while the program needs food before that date. A direct swap fails: the growers do not need the program's volunteer services at the same time, and the program cannot offer equivalent goods. A credit-and-reciprocity arrangement can work if Priya records it carefully.

Priya sets an initial 90-day cycle. She asks three growers to contribute produce during the first month and records each contribution at an agreed local value. In return, the program provides specific services rather than an undefined promise: volunteer labor at farm workdays, transportation assistance, and promotion at community distribution events. She assigns each service a stated value before anyone commits.

Her ledger contains these fields:

Field	Example
Contributor	Green Valley Farm
Present contribution	40 produce boxes
Agreed value	$600
Return obligation	12 labor hours and two delivery runs
Completion deadline	October 31
Review dates	August 15 and September 15
Change rule	Reschedule once with seven days' notice

Priya then follows the sequence. First, she works with growers who already know the program or have reliable references. Second, she defines what each side provides now. Third, she records the future service in hours and deliveries. Fourth, she schedules two review dates instead of waiting until the end. Fifth, she closes the obligation with a signed or acknowledged entry when each service occurs.

The program measures three outcomes over the 90 days. It tracks the value of food received, the number of promised service hours completed, and the number of obligations still open at the deadline. It also records cash impact: if the program would otherwise purchase $600 of food, the arrangement preserves that cash, but only if Priya completes the return services without creating overtime or transport costs that exceed the benefit.

Suppose the program completes all 12 labor hours but misses one delivery run. Priya should not treat the entire arrangement as successful. She should record the remaining obligation, agree on a replacement date, and assess the direct cost. If the missed run forces a $90 emergency delivery, the ledger should show that cost. This measurement prevents social goodwill from hiding a real financial loss.

After three months, Priya can classify the arrangement. If the growers received the promised value on time and the program preserved cash without disrupting its core work, the credit system created useful flexibility. If obligations repeatedly remained open, Priya should shorten the cycle, require partial payment, or limit future commitments to contributors with stronger records. The historical principle remains practical: trust may begin an exchange, but records and repayment keep it healthy.

Avoiding Mistakes in Credit-First Exchange

Treating goodwill as a repayment system

The root cause is a mistaken belief that a strong relationship removes the need for terms. Historical communities could rely on reputation because repeated contact and public knowledge created consequences. A modern arrangement may lack those controls, especially when volunteers, suppliers, and customers interact irregularly.

Do this: Record the contribution, the return obligation, the value, the deadline, and the review date before the exchange begins. Use a shared document when several people must see the same balance.

Not this: Do not rely on "we will make it right later." That phrase hides the amount, timing, and standard for completion.

Confusing delayed reciprocity with unlimited credit

The root cause is failure to set a limit. A community may support a member through one difficult season, but repeated advances can turn mutual aid into an uncollectible claim. A business can preserve cash through supplier terms, yet late payment can damage the relationship and interrupt supply.

Do this: Set a maximum open balance and a maximum time outstanding. Review the balance weekly for short arrangements and at agreed milestones for seasonal arrangements. Stop new commitments when the old obligation passes its limit.

Not this: Do not accept new goods or services simply because the other party has accepted earlier promises. A growing unpaid balance does not prove trust; it may show weak controls.

Measuring only the social benefit

The root cause is ignoring the cost of fulfilling the return. Priya's food program might receive valuable produce but spend more on transport, coordination, and labor than the cash it saves. Credit-first exchange still requires economic discipline.

Do this: Track both sides in the same unit where possible, then record extra costs in cash. Compare the value received with the actual cost of repayment and administration.

Not this: Do not call an arrangement successful because it feels cooperative. Reciprocity must improve access, timing, resilience, or cost without creating an obligation the organization cannot meet.

Quick reference: Use the Sequence Reversal Lens by checking the relationship first, defining what moves now and later, recording every obligation, setting a limit and review date, and measuring the full cost of repayment. Credit and social obligation often made exchange possible before barter could coordinate it. The same insight helps modern households and businesses preserve flexibility without confusing trust with wealth.

CHAPTER 6

Gift Economies and Delayed Reciprocity

When a Gift Becomes Working Capital

What would happen if your organization had the supplies it needed today, but the payment arrived only months later? Miguel, a 45-year-old nonprofit director, faced that problem when his community food program entered its busiest season with an empty reserve account. The program needed shelving, delivery van repairs, accounting help, and weekly produce. Cash could cover only one of those needs.

Miguel's usual answer - ask vendors for discounts - failed because the vendors also faced tight cash flow. A direct barter arrangement failed for a different reason: the mechanic did not need food, the accountant did not need shelving, and the farm could not use nonprofit event services at the moment. The old "double coincidence of wants" problem appeared in a modern office.

The program did have valuable resources. It had volunteers, meeting space, trusted relationships with local businesses, and a reliable ability to direct donated food to families. Miguel needed to convert those resources into present support without pretending that every exchange had to happen at once. The stakes were practical: if he could not keep deliveries running for twelve weeks, several partner stores would stop donating surplus food.

He treated gifts and delayed returns as an economic system rather than as informal favors. That distinction mattered. A gift creates an obligation, but the obligation does not always require an identical return, an immediate return, or a return to the original giver. Miguel's task was to record those obligations clearly enough that trust could support operations without turning into confusion or resentment.

How Miguel Built a Reciprocity Timeline

Miguel began by listing the program's needs for the next twelve weeks. He assigned each need a cash price, a deadline, and a consequence if it went unmet. A van repair cost $1,800 and had to happen within ten days. Produce deliveries required about $600 per week. Shelving cost $900 but could wait a month. Bookkeeping support cost $500 per month and could start immediately.

He then listed resources the nonprofit could offer. The organization could provide a partner grocery store with four volunteer shifts each month, allow a local accounting firm to use its training room for two evening workshops, and promote participating businesses through its donor newsletter. It could also direct surplus produce from one farm to a neighborhood kitchen, even when the farm could not receive a direct service in return.

To prevent vague promises, Miguel created the **Reciprocity Timeline**. He used a spreadsheet with six columns:

| Contribution | Recipient | Estimated value | Obligation created | Expected return window | Evidence of completion | |---|---|---:|---|---|---| | Four volunteer shifts | Grocery partner | $480 | Partner provides weekly produce | 30 days | Signed shift log and delivery records | | Training room access | Accounting firm | $300 | Firm provides bookkeeping hours | 14 days | Room-use record and

completed reports | | Surplus produce referrals | Farm | Variable | Farm contributes produce when available | Ongoing, reviewed monthly | Delivery log and invoice credit | | Donor newsletter placement | Repair shop | $250 | Shop discounts van repair | 10 days | Repair invoice |

The dollar figures did not turn every relationship into a purchase. They gave Miguel a common measuring stick. Without a reference value, one side could remember a generous contribution while the other remembered a small favor. The estimate also helped him avoid overpromising. If four volunteer shifts carried an estimated value of $480, Miguel could not responsibly promise them to three different partners.

The first turning point came with the van repair. A repair shop agreed to reduce the $1,800 bill by $600 if the nonprofit gave the shop a prominent newsletter placement and organized two volunteer cleanup days at the shop. Miguel recorded the $600 reduction as a contribution from the shop, not as free money. The nonprofit owed a defined return: two cleanup days within sixty days and one newsletter placement before the repair invoice came due.

The second turning point involved the farm. The farm did not need volunteer labor, advertising, or meeting space. Instead of forcing a direct exchange, Miguel created a three-party arrangement. The farm delivered surplus vegetables to the nonprofit. The nonprofit routed part of those vegetables to a community kitchen. The kitchen, which had a commercial freezer, stored prepared meals for the nonprofit's emergency distribution days. No party received an identical return from the party that first contributed value. The network worked because each participant accepted a useful return at a different time.

Miguel placed limits on the arrangement. He set a $2,000 maximum outstanding obligation for any one partner, required written confirmation for commitments above $500, and reviewed open obligations every Friday. He also separated gifts from exchanges. A donor who gave $1,000 without requesting a service appeared in the gift register. A business that supplied produce in return for future promotion appeared in the reciprocity ledger. Mixing both categories would have produced misleading financial records and damaged trust.

After six weeks, Miguel measured results against the original plan. The van repair finished on time. Produce deliveries continued for the full period. The accounting firm completed three months of bookkeeping, reducing the nonprofit's immediate cash requirement. Two obligations remained open, but both had scheduled completion dates. The system had not eliminated cost; it had moved some costs across time while making the promises visible.

Miguel also tracked failure points. One grocery partner missed a volunteer shift, so the nonprofit recorded a $120 shortfall and rescheduled the shift within two weeks. That small correction protected the larger relationship. Delayed reciprocity works only when participants can see what remains owed and resolve misses before they become evidence of bad faith.

What You Can Steal from Miguel's System

Treat a gift as an obligation with a different repayment rule. A gift does not mean "nothing is owed." It often creates a social or economic obligation, even when the return takes another form. Record the contribution, the recipient, and the agreed return window. If a supplier gives you materials worth $400, write down whether you owe payment, future work, a referral, or simply continued participation in a shared arrangement. This practice prevents two common errors: assuming generosity will continue forever and demanding an immediate, identical return that the giver never requested.

Use the Reciprocity Timeline to match value across time. Create one row for every significant contribution. Record the estimated value, the person or organization receiving it, the expected return window, and the evidence that proves completion. Review the sheet weekly. Set a limit on open obligations, such as $2,000 per partner or one month of expected service. The limit matters because delayed returns can accumulate faster than your ability to deliver them. A visible timeline turns goodwill into a manageable operating resource without confusing it with cash.

Allow three-party exchanges when direct barter fails. Do not reject a useful contribution because you cannot give the contributor what they need. Find another participant who can complete part of the exchange. Miguel's farm, nonprofit, and community kitchen formed a workable chain because each party valued a different result. For your own business or organization, map the exchange in three questions: Who can provide the resource? Who needs the resource? Who can provide the return that the first party actually wants? Write each handoff down before anyone commits. This method expands the pool of possible trades while preserving accountability.

Separate gifts, credits, and earned returns in your records. Use three labels: gift, credit, and exchange. A gift carries no specified service requirement, although it may create a broader relationship. A credit records value supplied now for a defined future benefit. An exchange records a specific return on a stated timeline. Keep these labels in separate spreadsheet tabs or accounting categories. The distinction protects your financial decisions. If you treat a conditional credit as unrestricted income, you may spend resources that someone else expects you to deliver later.

Measure whether delayed reciprocity actually improves your cash position. At the end of each month, compare three figures: cash preserved, obligations still open, and obligations completed on time. Suppose a delayed arrangement preserves $3,000 in cash but creates $4,500 of unpaid service commitments. The arrangement may have solved an immediate shortage while creating a future problem. Set a rule that open obligations must remain below a defined share of your monthly operating capacity. If your team can provide only forty volunteer hours next month, do not promise sixty hours because a partner supplied goods today.

Gift economies and delayed reciprocity do not replace disciplined finance. They reveal that value can move through a community before money changes hands, provided participants track obligations and respect timing. Miguel succeeded because he treated trust as an asset that required records, limits, and regular settlement. That same discipline helps explain why credit systems, currencies, and markets developed: people needed a reliable way to measure, transfer, and close obligations across distance and time.

CHAPTER 7

Silent Trade: Negotiating Without Contact

Choosing Contactless Exchange Without Losing Control

For thousands of years, traders have used a simple rule when direct contact created danger: leave goods at a neutral place, withdraw, and allow the other party to respond. Historians call this practice "silent trade" or "dumb barter." The name sounds primitive, but the underlying problem remains modern. A buyer and seller may need to exchange value while avoiding theft, pressure, disease exposure, border conflict, or disputes over who arrived first.

The decision matters because removing face-to-face contact removes useful information. You cannot immediately inspect the other party's goods, read their intentions, or negotiate a correction. A poorly designed exchange point can create more risk than a direct meeting. A well-designed one can separate the people from the transaction, create a clear record of performance, and reduce opportunities for intimidation.

Hana, a 26-year-old travel writer, faced this problem while arranging a local exchange of writing services for transport and lodging. She could meet the provider in person, send the work first through a digital channel, or use a neutral exchange point where each side deposited its contribution under agreed conditions. Her choice affected more than convenience. If she delivered a completed article before receiving transport, she carried credit risk. If she met an unknown provider alone, she carried personal-safety risk. If she used an unclear drop-off arrangement, she risked a dispute over timing, quality, or missing goods.

The right question is not, "Can I avoid contact?" It is, "Which exchange structure gives both sides a fair way to prove performance without creating unnecessary danger?"

Comparing Neutral Exchange Methods

Silent trade works when the parties agree in advance on four facts: what each side will provide, where each side will place it, when the exchange will occur, and what evidence will confirm completion. Without those details, a neutral site becomes only an unattended hiding place.

Approach	Cost	Time	Difficulty	Best for
Direct face-to-face exchange	Low to moderate	Fast	Low	Local trades where both parties can verify identity and goods safely
Digital escrow or payment hold	Low to moderate	Moderate	Moderate	Services, digital files, deposits, and transactions where a platform can release value after conditions are met
The Neutral-Site Protocol	Low	Moderate	Moderate	Physical goods or mixed exchanges where parties need distance, inspection rules, and a shared record

Direct exchange offers the fastest correction. If a tool arrives damaged, the buyer can reject it immediately. However, the same physical proximity that makes correction easy can create pressure. A seller may demand payment before inspection, or a buyer may dispute a condition after handling the item. Direct contact also exposes each party to information they may not want to share, such as a home address, travel schedule, or cash on hand.

Digital escrow reduces some of that risk by holding money or files until both parties meet defined conditions. It works especially well when the exchange involves an online service or a standard payment. It works less well when the parties exchange unusual physical goods, local services, or items that require judgment. A platform may not know whether a handmade product meets a quality agreement, and a release process may take longer than the trade itself.

The Neutral-Site Protocol provides a practical middle ground. It uses a public or controlled location, separate deposits, time-stamped evidence, and a written acceptance rule. A library locker, staffed parcel counter, hotel reception desk, workplace mailroom, or rented storage compartment can serve as the site. The best location does not merely sit halfway between the parties. It limits unauthorized access, protects the goods from weather, preserves a record, and gives both sides a clear deadline.

The protocol cannot eliminate every dispute. It can, however, narrow the dispute. Instead of arguing about intentions, the parties can examine whether Hana placed the agreed article in the specified folder by 4:00 p.m., whether the provider left the transport voucher in the assigned locker, and whether either party reported a defect within the inspection period.

The Verdict: Use the Neutral-Site Protocol When Contact Creates More Risk Than Value

If both parties can safely meet and inspect ordinary goods, choose direct exchange. It costs less time and allows immediate correction. If the transaction involves money, digital work, or a service that a platform can verify, choose escrow. The platform's rules matter because they define when one party earns release.

If the exchange involves physical goods, unfamiliar parties, travel, or a meaningful power imbalance, choose The Neutral-Site Protocol. Hana should not meet an unknown transport provider alone merely to exchange an article for a ride. She should use a staffed location, separate deposits, and a short inspection period. That arrangement protects her without making the trade unnecessarily expensive.

Use this decision flow:

- If you can verify identity, inspect both contributions, and leave safely, choose a direct exchange. - If money or digital work can sit with a trusted platform until conditions are met, choose escrow. - If either party needs physical distance, choose The Neutral-Site Protocol. - If the goods could spoil, lose value quickly, or attract theft, choose a staffed site with a short collection window. - If the other party refuses written terms, a neutral location, or evidence of deposit, stop the trade rather than redesigning the safeguards around their resistance.

The protocol also suits trades between groups that do not share strong social trust. Historically, silent trade often appeared between strangers or separate communities because direct bargaining could produce conflict. The neutral point acted as a boundary. Each side could make an offer without entering the other side's territory. Modern traders can apply the same logic to unfamiliar suppliers, online contacts, temporary travel arrangements, and exchanges involving personal safety.

A neutral site does not mean an anonymous site. Both parties should exchange enough identity information to enforce the agreement, while avoiding unnecessary disclosure. A staffed parcel counter may record the sender and recipient. A hotel desk may record the package number and collection time. A public locker may provide a code, but the parties still need a written record showing who controlled each code and when.

Making The Neutral-Site Protocol Happen

1. **Define the two contributions in observable terms.** Do not write "good transportation" or "professional writing." Write "one 1,200-word article in a shared document, with two original photographs, delivered by 4:00 p.m. Tuesday," or "one airport transfer from the central station to the airport, available between 6:00 and 6:30 a.m. Wednesday." Describe quantity, condition, deadline, and acceptable substitutes. Specific terms reduce the chance that one side treats a vague promise as complete performance.

2. **Choose a site that controls access.** Prefer a staffed reception desk, parcel counter, library locker, workplace mailroom, or secure storage unit. Avoid isolated paths, unlocked sheds, public benches, and locations exposed to rain or theft. Check the site's hours before agreeing to it. If the site closes at 5:00 p.m., do not set a 5:30 p.m. collection deadline. The site must remain available for the entire exchange window.

3. **Assign separate spaces or containers.** Give each contribution a clear location: locker 14 for Hana's article and photographs, locker 15 for the transport voucher. If the site offers only one compartment, use sealed packages with distinct labels and photographs. Separate placement prevents one party from taking the other contribution before depositing their own.

4. **Set the sequence and deadline in writing.** A workable rule might read: "Each party deposits its contribution by 4:00 p.m. Tuesday. Each party sends a photograph showing the sealed package and locker number. Neither party collects before receiving the other photograph.

Each party has until 8:00 p.m. Tuesday to report a missing or visibly damaged contribution." This sequence gives both sides evidence without requiring simultaneous physical presence.

5. **Use tamper evidence and time records.** Seal packages with numbered tape, a signed label, or a disposable security seal. Photograph the item, label, and location in one image. Include a clock, receipt, or site confirmation when possible. Digital timestamps do not prove every fact, but they establish a useful sequence. For higher-value goods, ask the site attendant to issue a receipt and record the package condition.

6. **Set an inspection and rejection rule.** The receiving party needs a reasonable opportunity to check the contribution. Hana could inspect the article for the agreed word count, required photographs, and basic factual accuracy within two hours of collection. She should report a specific failure, not simply say that she dislikes the work. The provider should inspect the article and voucher under the same rule. A rejection should identify the missing condition and state whether the contributor gets a short correction period.

7. **Define the remedy before the exchange.** If one side fails, decide what happens: return the goods, allow one correction, reduce the agreed value, or cancel the trade. For a perishable item, return may have no practical value, so the agreement may require a partial replacement or a credit toward a later exchange. A remedy gives both parties a reason to perform and prevents a small defect from becoming a personal confrontation.

8. **Keep a complete record.** Save the written terms, identity details, photographs, receipts, timestamps, and messages in one folder. Name files clearly, such as "Tuesday-deposit-Hana-1602" and

"Tuesday-collection-provider-1740." Records matter because memory compresses events after a dispute. A clear file lets both sides compare the agreement with what actually happened.

9. **Close the exchange deliberately.** Send a final message stating that both contributions arrived, passed inspection, or entered the agreed correction process. Delete access codes after collection and remove labels that expose travel plans, home addresses, or payment information. The exchange ends when both parties confirm completion, not merely when someone removes a package.

Use this checklist today:

- Write the exact quantity, condition, deadline, and inspection rule for your next contactless trade. - Select a staffed or controlled neutral site and confirm its opening hours. - Prepare separate labels, sealed packaging, and a method for time-stamped photographs. - Agree on the remedy for a missing, late, damaged, or incomplete contribution. - Store the agreement and evidence in one dated folder before either side deposits anything.

Silent trade succeeds through structure, not silence alone. The neutral point creates distance, but the written terms, controlled access, evidence, and remedy create trust. That lesson extends beyond physical barter: every market mechanism works better when participants can verify performance without relying entirely on personal contact.

CHAPTER 8

Mesopotamian Accounting Before Settlement

Why Tokens and Tablets Matter

"An unpaid obligation is still an entry in someone's account." That principle explains why Mesopotamian exchange did not require every transaction to end with coins, or even with an immediate delivery of goods. From roughly 3500 to 2000 BCE, clay tokens and cuneiform tablets helped record grain, livestock, labor, rations, taxes, and debts. The records tracked value across time, people, and goods.

This matters because barter becomes difficult when one party delivers today and receives payment later, or when a worker earns grain while a storehouse holds the supply. A token could represent a measured quantity. A tablet could identify who owed what, when the obligation arose, and whether the account had been settled. The system created a practical unit of account before modern money served that role.

The lesson applies to anyone who manages uneven exchanges. Ethan, a 52-year-old museum curator, may receive an artifact, arrange conservation work, and pay a specialist with stored materials or future services. If he records only the physical items, he loses track of the obligation. If he records the item, its agreed measure, the counterparty, and the settlement condition, he creates a reliable account. The Token-to-Trust Pipeline shows how to make that record clear.

Your Toolkit for Reconstructing Value

A unit-of-account sheet Define the measure that gives each item a common value, such as bushels of barley, liters of oil, days of labor, or kilograms of copper. Use a spreadsheet or paper ledger; both cost little or nothing, but the measure must remain consistent.

A transaction ledger Record the date, parties, item, quantity, agreed value, delivery status, and remaining balance. A basic spreadsheet works well and costs nothing through tools such as LibreOffice Calc or Google Sheets.

A token or marker system Use labeled counters, cards, or digital entries to represent specific goods or obligations. A physical token can cost only a few cents, while a digital record avoids storage problems; the important feature is clear identification, not the material.

A conversion table List the agreed relationship between goods and services. For example, one day of cataloging might equal two units of stored grain, while one conservation session might equal five units. Update the table only when both parties approve a new rate.

A verification record Attach a receipt, signature, photograph, inventory number, or witness note to each entry. Ethan can link a conservation charge to an artifact number and a signed service agreement, preventing a general promise from becoming an untraceable claim.

A settlement register Keep a separate list of open, partial, and closed obligations. This prevents a delivered item from being counted twice and shows whether an account still requires goods, labor, or a balancing adjustment.

A time-and-condition field Record when settlement must occur and what counts as acceptable delivery. "Ten units of grain" lacks the detail of "ten dry, measured units delivered by the first day of the harvest month."

The Token-to-Trust Pipeline

1. **Name the obligation.** Write exactly what one party provides and what the other party owes. Ethan records: "Museum receives one restored storage cabinet; conservator receives six labor units and two units of stored material." The outcome is a defined exchange rather than a vague promise.

2. **Choose one measuring unit.** Select a unit that both parties can verify. Use labor days, kilograms, liters, or another physical measure. Do not combine "a fair amount" with a numerical entry; the outcome must produce a quantity that another person can check.

3. **Assign a token to each claim.** Create one marker for each unit or obligation. If Ethan owes six labor units, he records six matching entries rather than one unexplained total. The outcome is a visible balance that can shrink as settlement occurs.

4. **Record the counterparty and date.** Enter who delivered value, who received it, and when the exchange began. Mesopotamian tablets often connected goods and obligations to institutions, officials, workers, or merchants; your record needs the same chain of responsibility.

5. **Separate delivery from settlement.** Mark an item as "delivered," "accepted," or "owed." A person can deliver work before receiving grain, or receive materials before completing a service. The outcome is a ledger that distinguishes possession from payment.

6. **Set a conversion rule.** State how one type of value converts into another. Ethan may agree that one cataloging day equals one labor

unit and that one labor unit can be settled with a specified quantity of stored grain. The outcome is a usable exchange rate rather than a later argument.

7. **Attach conditions to the entry.** Record quality, timing, location, and acceptable substitutes. "Two units of oil" should identify the type, container, and delivery point if those details affect value. The outcome is a claim that remains understandable after memory fades.

8. **Post partial settlement immediately.** Reduce the balance when the debtor delivers part of what they owe. If Ethan receives three of six labor units, his ledger should show three delivered and three open. The outcome is an accurate remaining claim.

9. **Verify the physical stock.** Compare the ledger with the goods on hand. Count containers, weigh materials, inspect condition, and reconcile differences. A tablet can preserve an obligation, but it cannot create grain, oil, or labor that does not exist.

10. **Close the account with evidence.** Mark the obligation settled only after both sides confirm completion. Add a date, signature, witness, or linked receipt. The outcome is a closed record that cannot be mistaken for an open debt.

11. **Review open claims on a fixed schedule.** Ethan checks the settlement register every Friday and flags any obligation older than its agreed due date. A regular review exposes shortages before they affect a budget, collection, or future exchange.

12. **Preserve the original and the correction.** If an entry changes, do not erase the first version. Add a dated correction that explains the reason. This practice preserves the history of the account and makes manipulation easier to detect.

Consider Ethan's museum exchange. A local workshop restores a cabinet in return for six labor units and two material units. Ethan records the cabinet's inventory number, the workshop's name, the delivery date, the agreed conversion table, and the remaining balance. The workshop completes the restoration, but the museum settles only four labor units immediately. The ledger therefore shows a completed delivery, four units settled, and two units still owed. When Ethan later provides the remaining value, he closes the account with a receipt. The record tracks value even though no coin changes hands.

The central discipline involves separating three questions: What changed hands? What did each item represent? What remains unpaid? Tokens answer the second question; tablets or ledgers preserve the answer over time. Together, they turn memory and trust into an auditable process.

Token-to-Trust Quick Reference

Unit of account - Choose one measurable standard before recording value. Use grain, oil, metal weight, labor time, or another unit that both parties can inspect.

Open obligation - Mark value as owed when one side has delivered but the other side has not completed settlement.

Partial settlement - Reduce the balance immediately after each delivery. Never wait until the entire exchange ends.

Conversion rule - Write the exchange relationship before work or delivery begins. If the rate changes, record the date and both parties' approval.

Proof of delivery - Attach a receipt, signature, inventory number, photograph, or witness note to each completed transfer.

Physical check - Compare recorded quantities with actual stock at least once each review cycle.

If the item has no shared measure, then do not record it as settled value. Agree on a unit first.

If delivery occurs before payment, then open a debt entry with a due date and conditions.

If the parties disagree about quality, then keep the obligation open and record the inspection result rather than closing the account.

If a balance changes, then add a dated correction instead of deleting the original entry.

If a claim lacks a named counterparty, then treat it as incomplete and investigate before relying on it.

If goods cannot settle the full obligation, then record the remaining balance separately from any substitute payment.

If the ledger and stock disagree, then stop new exchanges involving that item until you reconcile the difference.

Minimum record - Party, date, item or service, quantity, unit, delivery status, conversion rule, due date, and evidence.

Closing test - An account is settled only when the ledger, physical delivery, and both parties' confirmation agree.

Mesopotamian accounting demonstrates that money did not need to appear before people could measure, transfer, and enforce value. A well-kept token and tablet system made delayed payment visible and made trust less dependent on memory. The same logic remains useful today: record the unit, preserve the obligation, and let settlement - not assumption - close the account.

CHAPTER 9

Silver as Unit of Account

Why One Measure Can Survive Many Settlement Media

Fatima, a 33-year-old accountant, closes a month in which clients paid through bank transfers, silver coins, and service exchanges. Her records would become useless if she priced each transaction only in the thing that changed hands. A plumbing repair paid with silver still needs comparison with a repair paid through a bank transfer. Fatima needs one stable measuring language even when settlement takes several forms.

That distinction explains why silver could serve as a unit of account without serving as the only medium of settlement. A unit of account answers, "How much is this worth relative to other things?" A settlement medium answers, "What actually closes the obligation?" A market can use silver to express wages, rents, taxes, and debts while allowing payment through grain, labor, copper, credit, or another currency.

The practical problem involves more than ancient history. A modern business may quote prices in dollars, accept barter, settle invoices through bank transfers, and hold physical assets. Separating the measure from the payment method lets you compare offers, record obligations, and detect bad trades. By the end, you will be able to build a silver-based account system, convert different settlement media into one measure, and identify when a quoted price hides a transfer of value.

How Unit-of-Account Separation Works

Unit-of-Account Separation treats measurement and settlement as two linked but independent tasks. First, you state the obligation in a common unit. Second, you choose the asset or service that settles it. Third, you record the conversion between the stated amount and the payment received.

Ancient accounting systems demonstrate the importance of this separation. Mesopotamian tablets recorded rations, debts, and deliveries in standardized measures even though the underlying economy moved grain, livestock, labor, and other goods. Silver often supplied the comparison point. A worker might receive grain, while an obligation still appeared as a silver-denominated amount. The account remained comparable because the measure did not change with every delivery.

Use the framework through four rules:

1. **Choose one measuring unit.** Select silver by weight, such as one gram of fine silver, rather than an uncertain coin label. Weight gives the account a physical reference. If you use a coin, record its actual silver content and purity.

2. **Price the obligation before naming payment.** Write "40 grams of fine silver" before writing "payable in cash, grain, or labor." This prevents the payment method from quietly changing the agreed value.

3. **Record every conversion at an identified date.** Silver and other assets change relative prices. State the date and reference price used to convert grain, currency, or services into silver. Without a date,

the record cannot show whether a later payment met the original obligation.

4. **Separate settlement risk from measurement risk.** A silver-denominated invoice may remain clear even if the payer uses a currency that loses purchasing power. The account tells you what was owed; the settlement record tells you whether the payer delivered enough value.

Consider a repair priced at 12 grams of fine silver. The customer offers 3 kilograms of wheat instead. If wheat trades at 4 grams of silver per kilogram on the agreed date, the payment satisfies the invoice. If the market price falls to 2 grams before delivery and the agreement fixed the conversion date at delivery, the customer must provide 6 kilograms. The same unit of account produces different settlement quantities because the contract chose a different conversion rule.

This method also clarifies the difference between a silver price and silver payment. A merchant can quote a tool at 8 grams of silver and accept a bank transfer equal to that amount. The merchant has used silver as the measuring unit, not necessarily as the settlement medium. That practice reduces confusion when buyers and sellers use different payment systems.

Putting Unit-of-Account Separation Into Practice

Fatima wants to compare three invoices for accounting services. One client offers a bank transfer, another offers silver, and a third offers electrical work. She chooses fine silver as the common measure and records each offer before accepting any payment.

1. **Set the account unit.** Fatima defines one unit as one gram of fine silver. She uses a verified bullion dealer's published price to

convert modern currency into grams. She records purity separately because a coin containing one gram of alloy does not necessarily contain one gram of fine silver.

2. **Quote the service.** She prices a monthly bookkeeping package at 75 grams of fine silver. The quote states that the amount converts into the chosen settlement medium on the invoice date. This prevents a later dispute over whether the parties used the price at agreement, invoice, or payment.

3. **Convert each offer.** On the invoice date, the reference price places 75 grams of silver at $90. A bank-transfer client pays $90. A silver-paying client delivers 75 grams of verified fine silver. The electrical contractor offers work valued at $110, which equals about 92 grams under the same reference price.

4. **Test the result.** Fatima accepts the electrical work only if she needs it and can verify its market value. The offer exceeds the 75-gram invoice by roughly 17 grams, but that extra value may disappear if she must buy materials, arrange access, or wait two months for completion.

5. **Record settlement separately.** Her ledger shows the obligation as 75 grams, then identifies the settlement: $90 transfer, 75 grams of silver, or electrical work valued at 92 grams. This preserves comparability across clients and makes unpaid balances visible.

The expected outcome is a clean comparison rather than three unrelated transactions. Fatima can calculate revenue in one measure, assess whether each settlement met the invoice, and identify hidden costs. She also avoids treating a promised service as equal to delivered value.

Quick checklist

- Choose fine silver by weight as the account unit. - Record purity, weight, and the price source. - State whether conversion occurs at agreement, invoice, or payment. - Quote the obligation before discussing acceptable payment. - Convert every settlement medium into the same silver measure. - Deduct delivery costs, waiting time, taxes, and verification costs. - Record the obligation and the settlement on separate ledger lines. - Reconcile the account when the payment arrives, not when someone promises it.

The framework works especially well for barter because barter often disguises unequal timing. A service delivered today against goods promised next month creates a credit relationship. Silver measurement keeps the credit amount visible even when no silver changes hands. If the recipient agrees to 30 grams for work completed now, the ledger should show 30 grams owed until the goods arrive and pass inspection.

A modern currency can also settle a silver-denominated account. Suppose the silver reference price rises between invoice and payment. If the contract fixes the currency amount on the invoice date, the payer owes that fixed amount. If the contract fixes the silver quantity, the payer must deliver the currency equivalent on payment day. Neither rule is automatically correct; the parties must choose deliberately because each allocates price risk differently.

What to Watch For

Confusing a coin with a measure

A coin's name may suggest a fixed value while its weight, purity, or legal status changes. Two coins called the same thing can contain different amounts of silver. That difference destroys accurate comparison.

Do this: Record gross weight, purity, and fine-silver content. Use a scale and, for meaningful transactions, an independent purity test.

Not this: Treat every coin with the same name as one identical accounting unit.

Changing the conversion date after the deal

A silver-denominated contract becomes unstable when one party selects the most favorable exchange rate after the fact. The payer may choose a low silver price, while the recipient chooses a high one. Both positions can appear reasonable only because the agreement lacked a timing rule.

Do this: Write the conversion date, price source, and settlement deadline into the agreement. For a 75-gram invoice, specify whether the currency equivalent uses the invoice date or the payment date.

Not this: Write "pay the equivalent in currency" without defining equivalent.

Ignoring settlement quality

A promise to deliver grain, labor, or another service may carry more risk than physical silver or an immediate bank transfer. Spoilage, delay, transport, taxes, and verification can reduce the real value even when the quoted conversion looks generous.

Do this: Convert the promised settlement into silver only after subtracting direct costs and assigning a reasonable value to delay. If electrical work appears worth 92 grams but requires 10 grams of materials and several weeks of coordination, record its net value rather than its headline price.

Not this: Accept a larger nominal amount simply because the conversion table shows a larger number.

Unit-of-Account Separation gives markets a common measuring language without forcing every transaction through the same payment channel. Silver can measure the obligation while currency, goods, labor, or credit settles it. The discipline lies in recording the unit, timing, conversion, and settlement quality separately. Once those records remain distinct, barter stops looking like an unpriced exchange and becomes what it often was: a transaction organized around a shared measure, even when the final payment took another form.

CHAPTER 10

Egypt's Deben: Valuing Goods by Weight

The Deben and the Problem of Direct Exchange

A jeweler weighing a gold bracelet does not need a customer to bring an equal quantity of silver, grain, or labor. The jeweler needs a dependable way to state what the bracelet represents in value. Ancient Egypt's **deben** supplied that reference: a standardized unit of weight that allowed people to price goods against a common measure, even when no metal changed hands.

The deben did not function exactly like a modern coin. It served primarily as a unit of account. Egyptian records could express the value of grain, copper, livestock, tools, or services in deben of copper, silver, or gold. The quoted metal acted as the measuring standard; the parties could settle through goods, labor, credit, or another accepted item.

Key insight: a weight standard can coordinate prices without requiring direct metal payment. That distinction matters today because many business decisions still depend on a reference unit rather than immediate cash exchange. A jeweler, contractor, or trader can compare unlike goods more clearly when each price connects to a stable measure.

Caleb, a 38-year-old jeweler, faces this problem whenever he trades repair work for inventory. A supplier may offer gemstones, while Caleb offers setting and polishing services. Their goods differ, but a shared valuation unit can make the exchange precise. The Deben

Valuation Method treats the unit of account as a bridge between unlike assets.

Core Principles of the Deben Valuation Method

1. A unit of account separates pricing from payment.

Egyptian accounting could state that an item carried a value of so many deben of copper without requiring the buyer to hand over that copper. The deben answered the question, "How much is this worth relative to other things?" It did not necessarily answer, "What object must the buyer deliver right now?"

That separation reduces the double coincidence problem. Caleb does not need his supplier to want exactly the same quantity of polishing work that Caleb wants in gemstones. He can price both sides in the same unit, then agree on settlement through inventory, services, or a mixed exchange.

2. The reference metal must have a stated identity.

A deben represented weight, but the metal attached to the valuation mattered. One deben of copper did not carry the same purchasing power as one deben of silver. A clear record therefore needed more than the word "deben." It needed the reference metal and, where relevant, the quality.

The same rule applies to modern comparisons. Caleb should not write "the bracelet equals 20 units." He should record "the bracelet equals 20 copper-deben equivalents," or use a modern currency reference while explaining the conversion. Without the reference, the number looks exact but carries little meaning.

3. Standard weight makes unlike goods comparable.

A sack of grain, a bronze tool, and a day of skilled labor cannot exchange naturally in equal physical quantities. A weight unit gives each item a common denominator. The unit does not make the goods identical; it makes their quoted values comparable.

This principle helps Caleb test whether a proposed barter deal protects his margin. If a gemstone lot carries a value of 48 copper-deben equivalents and his repair work carries a value of 12 per week, he can see that the exchange requires four weeks of work before he accepts it as even.

4. Measurement requires verification, not trust alone.

A standard only works when participants can check the weight and quality. Egyptian trade depended on scales, recognized weights, and records. A dishonest counterparty could manipulate the metal, the scale, the purity, or the written conversion.

Caleb should therefore record the unit, inspect the goods, and preserve the calculation. The point does not involve historical ceremony. It protects against a modern version of the same error: accepting a quoted value without checking the underlying quantity.

A Practical Valuation Using Deben Equivalents

Caleb wants to acquire a parcel containing small sapphires from a supplier. The supplier asks for 48 copper-deben equivalents. Caleb proposes payment through jewelry repair services rather than direct cash or metal.

Assume the parties agree that one completed repair package - cleaning, resizing, and basic setting - equals 12 copper-deben equivalents. The parties also agree that the sapphires meet the stated grade and that both sides will record the exchange in writing.

1. **Define the reference unit.** Caleb writes: "All values use copper-deben equivalents as the unit of account." This prevents confusion with silver or gold valuation.

2. **Inspect and measure the goods.** Caleb checks the parcel's contents, stone count, stated grade, and visible defects. He records the supplier's quoted value of 48 units. If the stones differ materially from the description, he renegotiates before discussing payment.

3. **Price Caleb's service in the same unit.** Caleb assigns 12 units to one repair package. He bases that figure on the time, materials, and opportunity cost of the work. If a package takes six labor hours and consumes two units of materials, the 12-unit price must cover those inputs and leave a reasonable return.

4. **Convert the exchange into matching quantities.** Caleb divides the total goods value by the service value:

48 units ÷ 12 units per package = 4 repair packages.

The exchange therefore requires four completed packages, not an informal promise to "do some repairs later."

5. **Specify delivery and timing.** Caleb and the supplier record that Caleb will complete one package each week for four weeks. The supplier transfers the sapphires after the first package, or both parties use a deposit and delivery schedule they consider secure. The schedule matters because delayed services create credit risk.

6. **Record adjustments before work begins.** If Caleb discovers that one repair requires an expensive replacement clasp, the parties should price that added material separately. Caleb should not absorb the cost simply because the original agreement used a neat round number.

Item	Copper-deben equivalent	Quantity	Total
Sapphire parcel	48	1	48
Repair package	12	4	48
Balance after exchange	-	-	0

The table shows the central advantage of the method: both sides can settle a trade without transferring copper. The unit of account creates the comparison, while the actual settlement uses services and gemstones.

Caleb should also compare the barter arrangement with a direct purchase. Suppose the sapphire parcel would cost 48 units in a cash transaction, while each repair package would normally sell for 15 units to retail customers. Four packages therefore represent 60 units of potential sales. Caleb should accept the barter only if the stones' expected resale value, quality, and strategic usefulness justify giving up those services.

Choice	Immediate result	Main risk	Decision question
Four repair packages	Receives sapphires without cash payment	Loses time for higher-paying customers	Can the stones produce more than 48 units of value?
Direct purchase	Keeps repair capacity available	Uses cash reserves	Does preserving cash improve near-term returns?

The deben method clarifies the exchange, but it does not guarantee that the quoted values are fair. Caleb still needs to compare alternative uses of his labor and inventory. A common unit improves the arithmetic; judgment determines whether the trade builds wealth.

Troubleshooting Valuation Errors

Problem: The parties quote a number of deben without naming the reference metal.

Why it happens: Historical weight units can sound more precise than they are. A record may state "30 deben" while leaving the reader unsure whether the figure refers to copper, silver, or another standard. Modern traders make the same mistake when they compare "units" without defining what each unit represents.

Fix: Write the reference directly into the agreement. Caleb should use wording such as, "30 copper-deben equivalents, based on the agreed valuation schedule." He should record any quality assumption and state whether the unit measures gross weight, fine metal content, or an agreed accounting value. If the parties cannot define the unit, they do not yet have a usable price.

Problem: The quoted weight does not match the actual quality or quantity of the goods.

Why it happens: Weight alone cannot capture purity, condition, workmanship, or usefulness. A heavier copper object may have less practical value than a lighter, well-made tool. A gemstone parcel may meet its weight target while falling short on clarity or cut.

Fix: Separate measurement from inspection. Caleb should weigh what requires weighing, test or inspect quality, and attach a description to the valuation. For the sapphires, he should record stone count, grade, defects, and any treatment. He should reduce the agreed deben value when the goods fail the stated conditions, because the unit cannot correct a false description.

Problem: The calculation balances on paper but weakens the business.

Why it happens: Equal quoted values do not create equal economic outcomes. Caleb's four repair packages may consume weeks that he could spend on higher-margin work. The supplier may also value the services differently from retail customers, or the sapphires may take months to sell.

Fix: Calculate opportunity cost before accepting the exchange. List the labor hours, materials, scheduling delay, resale time, and likely selling price. Then compare the barter with a cash purchase and with the best alternative use of Caleb's capacity. If four packages normally generate 60 units in sales but the stones offer only 48 units of realistic resale value, Caleb should renegotiate the ratio or reject the trade.

The deben's lasting lesson lies in its modest function. It did not need to replace every object with metal. It needed to give traders a shared measuring stick. Once Caleb defines the reference, verifies the goods, converts both sides into the same unit, and checks the opportunity cost, barter becomes more than an improvised swap. It becomes a recorded comparison of claims on goods, labor, and future purchasing power. That habit - separating measurement from payment - leads directly toward the broader mechanics of money and modern asset markets.

CHAPTER 11

Commodity Standards That Blur the Line

When a Commodity Starts Acting Like Money

What makes a cow, a shell, a lump of salt, or a string of beads more than a useful object? The answer is not simply scarcity. A commodity begins to resemble money when people accept it not only for its direct use, but because they expect someone else to accept it later.

To examine that shift, gather a notebook, a calculator, and four reference objects or images: cattle, shell money, salt, and beads. You do not need to own the objects. The task requires comparison, not collection. Record each item's direct use, ease of transport, ability to divide into smaller units, durability, and social acceptance. Those features reveal why these goods sometimes worked as proto-money - objects that performed some monetary functions before states issued standardized coins or notes.

The key distinction matters for anyone building wealth today. A commodity can carry value without serving as money. A sack of salt may preserve purchasing power in one setting, while a rare shell may function as a payment unit in another. Neither becomes reliable money merely because people value it. Acceptance, measurement, and trust determine whether exchange can scale.

The Commodity-Money Continuum

The **Commodity-Money Continuum** tracks a commodity's movement from useful good to widely accepted exchange instrument. It has four practical levels:

Level	Main role	Example
Direct commodity	People want the item for its own use	Cattle for milk, meat, breeding, or labor
Valued payment good	People accept it partly because others value it	Salt used to settle obligations
Proto-money	People use it repeatedly to compare and transfer value	Shells or beads used in regular payments
Standardized money	Authorities or markets define units, quality, and legal acceptance	Minted coins or government currency

The continuum does not claim that every society followed one fixed sequence. Historical evidence shows several arrangements. Mesopotamian administrations recorded rations and debts in accounting units long before ordinary people used coins for every purchase. In other places, cattle, shells, salt, or beads circulated alongside credit, gifts, taxes, and personal obligations. The important point concerns function: these objects could perform one or more jobs associated with money without fully replacing other exchange systems.

Cattle show both the strength and weakness of commodity money. A herd stores value, reproduces, and provides food, labor, and status. Yet cattle require land, water, and care. You cannot easily divide one cow into small payments without destroying the asset. Transport also creates risk. A cow therefore works better as a unit for major transfers, marriage payments, fines, or wealth displays than for buying daily necessities.

Salt solves a different problem. People can divide it, transport it in manageable quantities, and use it directly to preserve food. Those features make salt more practical for routine settlement than cattle. Its weakness appears when quality varies. Wet salt, contaminated salt, and local abundance can change its value. A payment system based on salt needs agreed measures and reliable inspection.

Shells and beads demonstrate the importance of social agreement. Cowrie shells, for example, became payment objects across parts of Africa and Asia because communities recognized them, moved them through trade networks, and sometimes counted them in established quantities. Their direct use mattered less than their visibility, portability, and shared meaning. Beads could serve a similar role, especially when makers controlled color, shape, material, and workmanship. A bead string could communicate rank, record a transfer, or settle an obligation, but only within a community that understood its standard.

Use the continuum by asking five questions about each commodity:

1. **What problem does it solve directly?** Salt preserves food; cattle provide food and productive capacity; shells and beads may provide decoration or social meaning. 2. **Can people measure it consistently?** A counted shell is easier to measure than an animal. A bead string needs an agreed length, pattern, or count. 3. **Can people move it safely?** Shells and beads travel more easily than cattle. Salt travels well only when packaging and climate cooperate. 4. **Can people divide it without destroying its value?** Salt performs well; cattle perform poorly. 5. **Will an unrelated seller accept it tomorrow?** This question separates a valuable good from a proto-money instrument.

Consider a concrete exchange. Suppose Zoe, an archaeologist, records a coastal market where one large basket of salt exchanges for four bead strings. A bead string contains twenty uniform beads. A trader then accepts two strings for a woven mat. The market has created an informal price structure: one mat equals forty beads, and one basket of salt equals eighty beads. The beads now perform a unit-of-account function because traders use them to compare values. They also perform a medium-of-exchange function because the mat seller accepts them without wanting salt.

Now introduce quality problems. If one trader mixes ten small, damaged beads into a twenty-bead string, the apparent price remains forty beads, but the real payment falls. Sellers respond by inspecting strings, demanding a premium for high-quality beads, or refusing mixed strings. The market may then create recognized bead types, counted bundles, or marked lengths. Standardization moves the commodity closer to money.

The same logic applies to salt. If a basket normally contains ten kilograms of dry salt but a seller fills it with damp salt, the basket no longer represents a stable amount. Buyers must weigh it, discount it, or reject it. A simple weighing practice can increase trust, but it also adds tools, labor, and enforcement. Monetary systems grow more useful as they reduce these repeated disputes.

Try the Continuum With Four Commodities

Run a short comparison using four index cards labeled **cattle**, **salt**, **shells**, and **beads**. On each card, write a hypothetical local exchange value and then test how well the item performs under ordinary market conditions.

Use these starting assumptions:

- One cow represents 100 value units. - One basket of dry salt represents 10 units. - One string of twenty uniform shells represents 2 units. - One string of fifty uniform beads represents 5 units.

Treat "value units" as a comparison tool, not as a claim about any historical price. Your purpose is to expose the mechanics.

First, price a tool costing 7 units. The cow cannot divide cleanly, so the buyer needs credit, a second good, or a partial claim on the animal. Salt can provide 7 units only if the seller accepts seven-tenths of a basket or agrees to measure it. Shells require three strings plus one unit of another good. Beads require one full string plus two-fifths of another string. The exercise shows why smaller, countable commodities often support more frequent exchange.

Next, test storage. Assume one basket of salt loses 20 percent of its usable quantity because moisture enters the container. Its effective value falls from 10 units to 8. Assume five beads break in transit. If the string originally held fifty beads and the market accepts only complete strings, the owner may lose the full 5-unit payment even though most beads remain. Assume the cow gains value through breeding but requires continuing care. Each commodity stores value differently, and each carries a different cost.

Finally, test acceptance. Mark an item "accepted" only when a seller who does not need its direct use still takes it in payment. If the tool seller wants salt for food preservation, that exchange demonstrates commodity demand. If the seller accepts beads because another trader, tax collector, or supplier will accept them later, the beads function more like proto-money.

Zoe's expected outcome is a simple comparison sheet showing that no commodity wins every test. Cattle score strongly on productive value but poorly on divisibility and transport. Salt scores well on direct usefulness and divisibility but poorly on durability when stored badly. Shells and beads score strongly on portability and counting but depend heavily on social recognition and quality standards.

Completion check:

- You can state the direct use of each commodity. - You can explain how each item might serve as a payment good. - You can identify the feature that prevents each item from becoming universal money. - You can distinguish direct value from value based on expected acceptance.

Common Errors When Reading Proto-Money

Mistake: Treating "valuable" as identical to "money"

A commodity may command a high price because people need it, admire it, or expect it to become scarcer. That does not make it a payment instrument. A breeding cow stores wealth, but a shopkeeper may not accept one for a small purchase. A decorative bead may attract a collector but fail as a common unit of account.

Do this: Ask whether people accept the item from someone who does not want its direct use. Then check whether people count, measure, and transfer it repeatedly.

Not this: Assume that scarcity or prestige alone proves monetary function.

Mistake: Ignoring measurement and quality

Shells, salt, and beads can vary in size, weight, moisture, color, and workmanship. Without a shared standard, a stated quantity hides uncertainty. "One basket of salt" may describe a dry, full basket or a damp, loosely packed one. "One string of beads" may describe uniform beads or a mixed collection.

Do this: Record the unit, quality rule, and inspection method. For salt, specify weight and dryness. For shells or beads, specify count, size, and acceptable condition.

Not this: Compare commodities by name alone, as if every cow, shell, basket, or bead string carried the same value.

Mistake: Assuming a universal historical progression

Cattle did not automatically lead to shells, shells did not automatically lead to coins, and coins did not eliminate credit or barter. Communities combined payment goods with debt records, gifts, taxation, redistribution, and direct exchange. The same commodity could function as food, wealth, tribute, ornament, or payment depending on the setting.

Do this: Identify the institution supporting acceptance: a market network, a temple, a ruler, a trading community, or repeated relationships among households.

Not this: Draw a straight line from "barter" to "commodity money" to "modern currency" without examining who measured the item and who enforced the standard.

Cattle, shells, salt, and beads reveal a central fact about markets: money does not begin with an object's physical properties alone. It begins when people coordinate around those properties, create dependable measures, and trust future acceptance. That same test remains useful when you assess modern currencies, commodities, and other assets.

CHAPTER 12

When Money Fails: Barter's Return

What Makes Barter Return

During the 2008 financial crisis, barter exchanges and direct trade networks expanded as businesses faced tighter credit, slower payments, and less dependable cash flow. The important point is not the exact size of that expansion. The pattern matters: when money becomes difficult to obtain, difficult to move, or difficult to trust, people return to direct exchange.

Barter means trading goods or services directly without using money as the middle step. A freight company may move a shipment in exchange for vehicle repairs. A warehouse may release unused packaging in exchange for maintenance work. The parties still need to agree on value, timing, quality, and records, but neither party needs to make a cash payment at that moment.

Money failure does not always mean that a currency becomes worthless. It can mean a bank freezes transfers, a payment processor stops serving an account, a government restricts withdrawals, or a supply shortage makes cash less useful than a needed product. **Scarcity** occurs when people cannot obtain enough of a necessary good. **Collapse** describes a broad breakdown in payments, production, or distribution. **Blockade** means a physical, legal, or financial restriction prevents goods or money from moving through a normal route.

These conditions create different forms of pressure. Scarcity increases the value of useful inventory. Collapse damages the payment system itself. Blockade separates buyers from sellers even when both sides possess something valuable. Barter reappears because it can bypass part of the damaged system. It cannot create missing goods, remove transport risks, or solve every disagreement, but it can connect two parties who still have complementary resources.

The Failure-Trigger Checklist

The **Failure-Trigger Checklist** helps you identify whether a barter arrangement responds to a real disruption or merely disguises a weak deal. Start by locating the failed link. Ask whether the problem affects supply, payment, transport, or trust.

Scarcity usually appears first in specific goods rather than across the entire economy. A logistics company may have fuel, tires, or spare parts available while a local repair shop lacks cash but has the labor and equipment to service vehicles. Direct exchange becomes practical when each side holds something the other needs immediately. The trade does not depend on both parties wanting the same quantity. They can adjust the balance with a partial cash payment, a future service, or a written credit.

Collapse produces a different situation. During a banking disruption, a customer may have money recorded in an account but lack access to it. A business may have completed work but wait weeks for a payment processor to release funds. In that environment, barter preserves production by replacing a blocked payment with a direct settlement. The parties should still record a fair value, because tax reporting, inventory records, and future disputes do not disappear when cash does.

Blockade often makes barter local. A border closure, port interruption, sanctions rule, fuel shortage, or failed road can prevent ordinary trade between regions. A business may possess excess inventory on one side of the restriction while another business faces an urgent shortage on the other. Direct exchange can work only if the parties can move the goods legally and safely. Barter does not excuse customs rules, sanctions, licensing requirements, or transport restrictions.

Use the checklist in this order:

1. **Name the failure.** Write down the exact obstruction: unavailable stock, frozen payment, blocked route, unreliable currency, or damaged trust. If you cannot identify the obstruction, you cannot judge whether barter addresses it.

2. **Measure the urgency.** Separate essential goods from convenient goods. A truck tire needed to keep a delivery fleet operating has a different exchange value from surplus office furniture. Record the deadline, quantity, quality requirement, and replacement cost.

3. **List what each party can deliver.** Include inventory, labor, equipment time, storage, transport, and future service. Avoid treating promises as equal to goods already in hand. A confirmed spare part deserves more weight than an uncertain promise of a later delivery.

4. **Set a reference value.** Check recent cash prices, replacement cost, and local availability. If a repair normally costs $600 and the available replacement part costs $400, the parties can structure a $400-for-$600 trade only if the extra service has a clear reason and both sides accept it.

5. **Test the route and the rules.** Confirm ownership, condition, delivery access, insurance, taxes, licensing, and legal restrictions. A

trade that violates transport or customs rules creates a larger loss than the original shortage.

6. **Write the settlement terms.** State what changes hands, when delivery occurs, how the parties inspect quality, what happens after a failure, and whether either side owes a remaining balance. A simple written agreement protects the trade when memory and trust face pressure.

A useful analogy comes from emergency power. A generator does not replace the electrical grid permanently; it keeps essential equipment running while the grid fails. Barter serves a similar role. It provides a temporary payment route when the normal route cannot carry the transaction. The closer the trade stays to an essential need, a verified resource, and a short settlement period, the lower the risk.

The checklist also exposes bad barter. A seller may offer unwanted inventory at an inflated value because cash buyers disappeared. A buyer may promise future labor without the capacity to deliver it. Both parties may call the arrangement "equal" while ignoring storage, transport, taxes, or quality. Those errors become more dangerous during disruption because replacements take longer and disputes consume scarce time.

Applying the Checklist to a Blocked Supply Route

Ravi, a 44-year-old logistics manager, oversees regional freight movement for a company that operates delivery vehicles and a small warehouse. A disruption closes the company's usual supply route for several weeks. The company still has customer shipments to complete, but its tire supplier cannot deliver on schedule. Ravi's fleet has enough fuel for current routes, yet two vehicles need replacement tires before they can safely operate.

A nearby commercial tire shop has the required tires in stock. The shop also needs warehouse space for a seasonal shipment and lacks enough room to hold incoming inventory. Ravi's company has unused storage capacity because several customer orders remain delayed. This creates a practical exchange: storage service for tires.

Ravi applies the Failure-Trigger Checklist rather than accepting an informal promise.

1. He identifies the failure as a blocked supply route, not a total money failure. The parties can still use cash, but cash alone cannot obtain tires through the normal supplier.

2. He measures the need. Two vehicles require tires within five days. Ravi confirms the tire size, load rating, condition, warranty, and installation requirement. He rejects a cheaper offer for tires that do not meet the vehicles' specifications.

3. He values both sides. The tire shop quotes $1,800 for the two tire sets and installation. Ravi checks the company's normal storage rate and calculates that three weeks of secure storage for the shop's incoming shipment would normally cost $1,500. The parties agree that Ravi's company will provide three weeks of storage plus $300 in cash. The cash balance matters because it prevents the storage service from carrying an inflated value merely to make the exchange appear equal.

4. He checks the route and rules. Ravi confirms that the tires have lawful ownership, that the storage facility's insurance covers the goods, and that the warehouse can accept the shipment without violating an existing customer contract. He also confirms that the tire shop can provide an invoice showing the agreed value.

5. He writes the terms. The agreement states the storage dates, pallet count, access hours, liability for damage, tire specifications, installation date, payment balance, and remedies if either party fails to perform. Ravi schedules tire installation before the storage period begins.

The trade keeps two vehicles operating and gives the tire shop usable warehouse capacity. It does not solve the blocked route. It buys time and preserves productive capacity while the normal supply channel remains unavailable. Ravi also records the transaction in the company's books at the agreed value, because a noncash exchange still affects revenue, expenses, inventory, and taxes.

Condition	Best barter resource	Main risk to check
Specific shortage	Verified inventory or repair labor	Wrong quality or inflated value
Payment disruption	Immediate goods or completed services	Delayed delivery or weak records
Transport blockade	Local storage, fuel, equipment, or supply	Illegal or unsafe movement
Currency distrust	Useful goods with clear local demand	Rapid value changes

Ravi's example shows why timing matters. If he waits until both vehicles fail, the tire shop gains bargaining power and the company may lose delivery revenue. Early identification creates more choices: storage, transport capacity, maintenance work, or a mixed trade with a smaller cash balance. Barter works best before the crisis reaches its most desperate stage.

Lessons From Barter Under Pressure

Takeaway: Barter returns when a specific link fails, not only when an entire economy collapses. A blocked payment account, missing spare part, or closed transport route can create a barter opportunity even while the wider currency remains usable. Identify the broken link first. Then ask whether direct exchange bypasses that link without creating a larger legal, safety, or delivery problem.

Takeaway: Useful goods outrank nominal value during scarcity. A warehouse space, working tire, fuel delivery, or skilled repair may matter more than an equivalent amount of unwanted inventory. Price the trade against replacement cost, urgency, and actual use. Do not accept a high stated value for something that cannot solve the immediate constraint.

Takeaway: Records become more important when money becomes less reliable. Direct exchange still creates obligations, taxable values, delivery risks, and disputes. Write the terms, record the agreed value, inspect the goods, and define failure remedies. Clear records turn an improvised exchange into a controlled transaction.

Key actions: identify the exact failure, separate essential needs from conveniences, verify what each party can deliver now, compare values with current cash prices and replacement costs, check legal and transport limits, and document every term. Barter is not a substitute for a functioning monetary system. It is a recovery tool that becomes valuable when scarcity, collapse, or blockade interrupts the usual path from need to payment. Used carefully, it keeps productive resources moving until ordinary market channels regain their function.

CHAPTER 13

Weimar Hyperinflation and Substitution Trading

> "When money loses its measuring function, people do not stop trading. They change what they use to measure value."

Currency Breakdown Changes the Exchange Channel

Weimar Germany shows how quickly ordinary trade can move away from official money. During the hyperinflation of the early 1920s, prices changed so rapidly that sellers struggled to keep shelves labeled, wages lost purchasing power between paydays, and buyers rushed to exchange cash for goods. The central problem did not involve a lack of goods alone. Currency stopped performing its basic jobs: it no longer measured value reliably, preserved purchasing power, or supported delayed payment.

That breakdown produced substitution trading: people replaced money with other exchange channels. They used foreign currency, stable goods, direct barter, credit, advance payment, and personal networks. A baker might prefer coal, flour, or a foreign note over domestic marks. A worker might spend wages immediately on food rather than hold cash until the next day. A business might quote prices in a more stable unit while accepting payment in several forms.

The important lesson concerns behavior, not nostalgia for barter. When money becomes unreliable, market participants search for a substitute that solves the immediate problem. The substitute must help them price goods, settle transactions, or preserve value. The

Substitution Spiral begins when one group abandons the currency, another group follows, and each replacement makes the official money less useful.

You need three distinctions before applying this idea. A **medium of exchange** helps people complete a purchase. A **unit of account** gives the price a common measure. A **store of value** carries purchasing power into the future. A single currency normally performs all three jobs. During hyperinflation, people may replace each function separately: foreign currency for pricing, goods for saving, and barter or credit for settlement.

The Substitution Spiral in Practice

The Substitution Spiral usually develops through connected stages rather than one sudden decision.

Stage 1: Sellers shorten their price horizon. A shop that once changed prices monthly may begin checking replacement costs daily or even several times a day. The seller does not raise prices simply because of fear. The seller raises them because the next shipment will cost more, and selling today at yesterday's price may prevent restocking tomorrow.

Stage 2: Buyers spend cash faster. Once households expect prices to rise sharply, holding domestic currency becomes costly. They convert wages into food, fuel, clothing, tools, or foreign notes as soon as possible. This behavior increases the speed at which money changes hands. Faster circulation adds pressure to prices because sellers receive cash and immediately try to exchange it again.

Stage 3: Traders quote value in a substitute unit. A business may think in foreign currency, gold, a commodity, or replacement cost while still accepting domestic money at the current conversion rate. The quoted price then reflects the substitute, not the paper currency. A repair job might carry a mark price that changes whenever the price of imported parts changes.

Stage 4: Settlement moves outside money. If currency cannot preserve value between agreement and payment, parties shorten payment terms or use direct exchange. A contractor may accept building materials, food, fuel, or a foreign note. A supplier may require payment before delivery. A customer may offer labor or another service instead of waiting for cash to lose value.

Stage 5: Credit contracts shrink. Credit becomes dangerous when the lender cannot predict what repayment will buy. Sellers demand immediate payment, collateral, or a price linked to a stable reference. This shift affects small businesses first because they often lack reserves and cannot absorb a loss between sale and replacement.

Stage 6: The substitute becomes a network. A single barter deal does not replace a currency. Repeated use does. Once several suppliers, workers, and customers accept the same alternative, that alternative gains practical value. The network reduces the need for a perfect "double coincidence of wants," because participants can trade through a trusted group rather than find one person who wants exactly what they offer.

Track the spiral through four measures: how often prices change, how long sellers allow payment terms to run, what share of transactions uses non-cash settlement, and how quickly the business converts domestic currency into stock or stable assets. Review these measures weekly during severe currency stress. Daily review may become necessary when replacement costs change within the same business day.

A substitute does not need to become a universal currency. It only needs to solve a specific failure. A foreign note may price imported equipment. Fuel may settle a local transport obligation. A written credit balance may support exchange among trusted businesses. Direct barter may work when both parties can value the goods and complete delivery promptly.

Sofia's Substitution Trading Plan

Sofia, a 27-year-old economics student, studies the Weimar episode while running a small tutoring service. Her students pay monthly, but her rent, transport, and food costs rise before she can spend the income. She decides to test substitution trading without pretending that barter can replace every financial need.

She begins with a simple record for four weeks:

Measure	Week 1 starting point	Target after four weeks
Days between earning and spending income	14 days	2 days
Payment terms offered to clients	30 days	7 days
Transactions settled partly without domestic currency	0	3 recurring arrangements
Cash reserve held in unstable currency	Full monthly surplus	Only near-term expenses

The figures describe her operating choices, not a prediction about any particular currency crisis. Sofia's purpose is to reduce exposure to rapid loss of purchasing power while keeping her service practical.

1. Separate pricing from settlement. Sofia prices each tutoring package by the replacement cost of her time and essential expenses. She reviews the price every Monday and whenever transport or food costs change materially. She avoids promising a fixed monthly price for several months because that would transfer all currency risk to her.

2. Shorten the payment window. She asks new clients to pay weekly rather than monthly. Existing clients receive a seven-day payment period. The shorter period matters because a delayed payment buys fewer goods if prices rise quickly. Sofia records the agreed service, delivery dates, and payment deadline in writing.

3. Create useful exchange options. Sofia accepts domestic currency, selected goods, or services only when she can value and use them. One arrangement exchanges tutoring for groceries delivered each week. Another exchanges tutoring for bicycle repairs. She rejects vague promises such as "help later," because unclear claims create disputes and do not protect purchasing power.

4. Use a reference price. For each barter arrangement, Sofia records the normal cash price at the time of agreement and the exact quantity of the substitute. If one tutoring session normally costs the equivalent of two grocery baskets, both parties write down what counts as a basket. This prevents one side from changing the terms after delivery.

5. Convert surplus promptly. Sofia keeps enough domestic currency for several days of transport and food. She uses additional income quickly for necessary supplies rather than holding it for a month. She does not treat every physical good as a safe asset; perishable goods, storage costs, theft, and quality loss can erase their apparent protection.

6. Review results every Sunday. After four weeks, Sofia compares completed sessions, missed payments, replacement costs, and disputes. A successful arrangement should reduce payment delays without consuming more time in negotiation than the service deserves. If a barter exchange takes an hour to arrange for a small tutoring fee, the channel fails even if no cash changes hands.

Her expected outcome is modest and measurable: faster settlement, fewer unpaid balances, and less exposure to rapidly falling currency value. She does not expect groceries or bicycle repairs to provide a universal store of wealth. She uses them because they meet immediate needs and because both parties can verify their value.

The plan also reveals a limit. Sofia still needs money for rent and obligations that landlords or public authorities do not accept in kind. Substitution trading works best as a layered system: use the most reliable channel for each payment rather than force every transaction into barter.

Errors That Break Substitution Trading

Treating every physical good as money

The root cause is confusion between usefulness and liquidity. A good may hold practical value but remain difficult to store, divide, transport, or resell. A large quantity of food can spoil; fuel can create safety problems; tools may have a narrow market.

Do this: Choose substitutes that match a known obligation, record their quantity and condition, and keep only what you can use or exchange within a reasonable period.

Not this: Buy random goods because prices are rising and assume someone will accept them later.

Ignoring the unit of account

The root cause is focusing on what changes hands while ignoring how both parties measure the deal. Without a shared reference, a barter agreement can look fair at signing and unfair at delivery.

Do this: Write the cash-equivalent reference, the substitute quantity, the delivery date, and the adjustment rule. Review the reference when replacement costs change.

Not this: Agree to "a few hours of work for supplies" without defining the work, supplies, timing, or quality.

Offering long credit in a collapsing currency

The root cause is treating a promise to pay as if it carried the same value as immediate payment. During rapid inflation, the borrower may repay exactly the stated amount while the lender receives far less purchasing power.

Do this: Shorten payment terms, request deposits, link repayment to a clearly defined stable reference, or accept useful goods and services at the time of delivery.

Not this: Keep ordinary thirty-day terms because they worked under stable prices.

Quick reference: When currency loses reliability, separate pricing from settlement, shorten the time between agreement and payment, and select substitutes for specific needs. Measure price-change frequency, payment delays, non-cash settlement, and currency exposure each week. The Substitution Spiral explains why these choices spread: once money fails one function, people replace that function first, then build exchange networks around the alternatives. Wealth preservation depends less on clinging to one medium than on recognizing which exchange channel still works.

CHAPTER 14

Prisons, Wartime Shortages, and Blockades

When Money Stops Moving

Victor, 39, worked as an aid worker in a coastal city placed under blockade after an armed conflict disrupted fuel deliveries, banking services, and commercial imports. The city still contained food, tools, medicine, and skilled workers, but the normal exchange system had fractured. Shops could not restock reliably. Banks opened irregularly. Electronic payments failed when electricity or communications failed. Cash remained useful, yet cash alone could not bring fuel through a closed checkpoint or replace a missing shipment of antibiotics.

The immediate problem involved more than scarcity. The city held resources in the wrong places. A clinic needed diesel for its refrigerator and generator. A mechanic had diesel but lacked flour. A bakery had flour but needed replacement belts for its mixer. A farming cooperative had vegetables but needed transport. Each participant possessed something valuable, but ordinary money markets could not connect supply with demand.

The stakes rose quickly. If the clinic lost refrigeration, medicines could spoil. If the bakery stopped, households would lose a dependable food source. If transport failed, vegetables would rot while neighboring districts faced shortages. Victor's team had to create a working exchange network without pretending that barter could solve every problem. They needed a system that identified what people had, measured what they needed, reduced disputes, and protected scarce supplies from waste and abuse.

The situation illustrates the **Constraint-Driven Market Model**: when movement, money, or trust becomes constrained, people reorganize exchange around available goods, services, relationships, and enforceable records. Informal markets do not appear because people suddenly reject money. They appear because money cannot complete the transaction by itself.

How Victor Built an Exchange Network

Victor began with an inventory rather than a marketplace. His team visited the clinic, bakery, mechanic, farming cooperative, and several transport operators. They recorded four facts for each participant: available supply, urgent need, location, and acceptable exchange terms. They also marked expiration dates and transport requirements. A box of vegetables available for two days required different treatment from a generator part that could remain useful for months.

The team used a simple ledger on paper and on a shared spreadsheet when communications allowed. Each entry included the item, quantity, quality, owner, location, date recorded, and whether the owner could release it immediately. This prevented a common failure in emergency exchange: counting promised goods as if those goods already existed. Victor classified supplies into three groups:

- **Immediate-use goods:** food, fuel, clean water, and medicine. - **Production goods:** tools, spare parts, seeds, and packaging. - **Services:** transport, repairs, medical work, storage, and labor.

The classification mattered because each group required a different exchange rule. Immediate-use goods needed rapid movement and close inspection. Production goods required a clear estimate of future usefulness. Services needed a time record and a defined result.

Victor's first successful match connected the clinic, mechanic, and bakery. The mechanic agreed to repair the bakery's mixer in exchange for a measured quantity of flour and a smaller fuel allocation. The bakery transferred flour only after the mixer passed a test run. The clinic then assigned the mechanic a fuel voucher backed by a verified diesel reserve. The voucher did not function as unrestricted money. It represented a specific claim against a specific stockpile, with a stated expiration date.

That distinction protected the network. A general promise such as "fuel later" could circulate beyond the issuer's ability to honor it. A claim for "20 liters of diesel from the clinic reserve, redeemable before Friday" gave the recipient something concrete to evaluate. Victor's team recorded every voucher and limited issuance to confirmed inventory. They also prevented double counting: once the mechanic received the fuel claim, the clinic marked that portion of its reserve as committed.

The next turning point involved the farming cooperative. It had vegetables but no dependable vehicle. Victor matched it with a transport operator who needed repair work on a truck. The mechanic repaired the truck in return for a weekly vegetable allocation. The transport operator then moved vegetables to the bakery and clinic. The team did not force a single three-way barter transaction. Instead, it linked separate exchanges through records. This created a small clearing system: participants could trade with the party that had what they needed, while the ledger tracked obligations across the network.

Victor set exchange terms using replacement difficulty rather than ordinary retail prices. Fuel received a high priority because no local substitute existed. Vegetables received a lower unit value per kilogram but moved quickly because they spoiled. A repair received a value based on labor time, parts consumed, and the cost of finding another mechanic. These were not permanent prices. They were working terms designed to move essential goods while conditions changed.

The team checked the network twice each day. At the morning check, they updated available stock and transport routes. At the evening check, they reconciled completed trades, canceled unavailable offers, and flagged disputes. Victor required confirmation from both sides before marking an exchange complete. For goods, confirmation required quantity and condition. For services, it required a defined completion standard. A truck repair counted as complete only after the vehicle operated under load, not merely after the mechanic declared the work finished.

The network also needed boundaries. Victor prohibited exchanges involving stolen goods, controlled medicines outside authorized channels, weapons, and promises unsupported by recorded assets. He separated emergency allocation from ordinary exchange. The clinic could receive fuel through a priority rule when patient safety required it, but the rule had to remain visible. Without such limits, the strongest negotiators could capture supplies while quieter participants disappeared from the network.

After several weeks, the system had become more than direct barter. It combined barter, credit, vouchers, labor records, and trusted intermediaries. Money still entered where available, but it no longer carried the entire burden of exchange. The system worked because Victor's team treated constraints as design conditions. They asked what could move, what could be verified, what could expire, and what obligation someone could realistically honor.

What the Constraint-Driven Market Model Teaches

Map assets before negotiating terms. Begin with a four-column inventory: available now, needed now, available later, and unavailable. Add quantity, location, condition, and expiration date. Victor's team could create useful matches because it knew that the city held flour, diesel, repair skills, and transport capacity in different places. A vague request for "more supplies" would not have revealed the bakery's specific need for a mixer belt or the clinic's need for fuel before a particular date. For a small business, the same method means listing unused stock, spare capacity, customer credits, and services you can exchange without damaging your cash position.

Match the exchange instrument to the constraint. Use direct barter when two parties want each other's goods immediately. Use a recorded credit when timing differs. Use a restricted voucher when the claim must attach to a specific reserve. Use a labor record when a service creates value but no physical item changes hands. Victor's fuel voucher worked because the clinic backed it with identified diesel and limited its redemption period. Do not issue general credits merely because people want a convenient substitute for money. If you cannot explain what backs the claim, who can redeem it, and when it expires, you have created a dispute rather than liquidity.

Value scarcity by replacement difficulty and time. A unit of exchange should reflect what happens if the item disappears. Victor treated fuel as more urgent than vegetables because the city could not replace fuel locally, while vegetables could return with the next harvest. He also moved perishable goods quickly instead of holding them for a theoretically better trade. Apply a simple test: ask how soon the item expires, how far the nearest substitute sits, and what operation stops without it. Record the answer beside each offer. This prevents a common barter mistake - trading according to familiar retail prices while ignoring the conditions that actually determine value.

Record obligations as carefully as physical goods. Informal markets fail when participants count promises, stock, and completed exchanges as the same thing. Keep a ledger with the issuer, recipient, asset backing, quantity, redemption date, and completion status. Reconcile it at a fixed time each day or week. Victor's team marked committed diesel as unavailable for further promises and required both parties to confirm completed trades. A tradesperson or shop owner can use a shared spreadsheet, numbered paper receipts, or accounting software. The tool matters less than the discipline of updating it immediately and canceling offers when conditions change.

Protect the network with visible rules and priority claims. Scarcity creates pressure to favor friends, powerful buyers, or whoever arrives first. Publish rules for essential goods, verification, dispute handling, and prohibited exchanges. Give priority to life-preserving uses only when the network can explain and review that decision. Victor separated clinic fuel from ordinary bargaining while still recording every allocation. In your own network, define which orders receive priority, what evidence supports a shortage claim, and who can approve an exception. Clear rules preserve trust, and trust allows strangers to exchange when normal institutions cannot.

Constrained markets reveal a basic fact about wealth: value does not disappear when currency fails, but exchange requires a structure that can identify, measure, and verify it. Barter networks become durable when participants treat goods, skills, promises, and access as distinct assets rather than as interchangeable favors. That discipline connects ancient exchange practices with modern questions about money, liquidity, and the assets people rely on when familiar markets stop moving.

CHAPTER 15

Countertrade and Corporate Barter Today

The Decision: Trade Goods, Credit, or Cash?

When a shipment of machinery reaches a port but the buyer cannot obtain enough dollars, euros, or another widely accepted currency, the transaction does not automatically fail. The buyer may offer local products, future deliveries, or access to a domestic market instead. That arrangement falls under **countertrade**: an international sale linked to a reciprocal purchase, resale obligation, or non-cash settlement.

Mina, a 36-year-old trade compliance officer, sees the central problem clearly. A seller may hear "we can pay with local goods" and focus on preserving the sale. Mina first asks a harder question: can the proposed goods be sold, valued, transported, insured, and legally imported without destroying the margin? A shipment of coffee, copper, fertilizer, or manufactured parts may have a market price, yet still produce a poor settlement if quality varies, export permits take months, or the seller lacks buyers.

The choice matters because countertrade replaces one simple payment obligation with several linked obligations. A cash sale usually ends when the buyer pays. A countertrade contract may require the seller to accept goods, resell them, meet quality standards, arrange freight, satisfy customs rules, and absorb currency or price risk. If the parties choose the wrong structure, a transaction that appears profitable can consume working capital and create an inventory problem.

The **Contractual Barter Engine** provides the practical test. Treat the proposed exchange as an economic system with four connected parts: the original sale, the reciprocal obligation, the conversion of goods into usable value, and the legal controls that keep both sides accountable. The system works only when each part has a defined price, deadline, owner, and remedy.

Comparing Countertrade Structures

International countertrade takes several forms. The right choice depends on how much hard currency the buyer can access, how easily the offered goods can move through established markets, and whether the seller wants inventory or only a reliable payment claim.

Approach	How it works	Cost	Time	Difficulty	Best for
Counterpurchase	The seller supplies goods for cash, then agrees to buy specified goods from the buyer's country	Medium to high	Months to several years	High	Established exporters with purchasing or resale capacity
Barter exchange	Both sides exchange goods directly, with limited or no cash settlement	High if goods need resale	Often slower than cash trade	High	Standardized commodities with transparent prices
Buyback	The seller supplies equipment or a plant and accepts output from that facility as payment	Very high	Several years	Very high	Industrial projects where the seller understands the output market
Offset or local-content agreement	The seller commits to local purchases, production, training, or investment linked to a major sale	High	Multi-year	Very high	Large government or infrastructure contracts

Counterpurchase often offers the most workable structure for a commercial exporter. The seller completes the main sale for at least partial cash, then purchases goods through a separate but connected agreement. For example, a machinery exporter might sell equipment for 70 percent cash and accept a commitment to purchase processed agricultural products for the remaining commercial value. The exporter can then sell those products through a broker instead of placing them directly into its own operations.

Barter appears simpler because the parties exchange goods directly. In practice, it creates the sharpest valuation problem. If one side delivers industrial pumps and the other delivers metal, the contract must define grade, inspection, delivery point, freight responsibility, and the price used to calculate equivalence. A published commodity price may provide a starting point, but it rarely settles differences in purity, packaging, location, or delivery date.

Buyback creates the longest exposure. A company that builds a processing plant and accepts part of its future output must assess construction risk, operating performance, commodity prices, and political conditions. The seller may receive valuable output, but it also becomes exposed to the buyer's ability to run the facility. This structure suits specialized industrial transactions, not ordinary small-business exports.

Offset agreements can involve local sourcing, technology transfer, or domestic production commitments. They often appear in large public contracts because the buyer wants broader economic benefits, not merely imported equipment. A smaller exporter should approach this structure cautiously. Compliance reporting, local-partner review, and long-term purchasing obligations can cost more than the original sales margin.

The most important distinction does not appear in the table: **who controls the conversion of goods into value?** If the seller already has a distribution channel for the reciprocal goods, counterpurchase may work. If the seller must locate buyers after receiving unfamiliar inventory, the arrangement needs a discount, a specialist intermediary, or a cash alternative. Never treat the face value of goods as equal to cash value until a real buyer, realistic delivery cost, and enforceable quality standard support that conclusion.

The Verdict: Use a Cash-Plus-Counterpurchase Structure First

For most businesses entering a hard-currency-constrained market, start with **counterpurchase supported by partial cash**, not pure barter. Require enough cash to cover production, freight, insurance, taxes, and a reasonable operating margin. Link the remaining obligation to goods that have a documented market and a clearly defined resale route. This structure reduces the amount of inventory risk while giving the buyer a way to complete the transaction.

If the buyer can pay the full price in a stable currency within the agreed period, choose the cash sale. If the buyer has limited currency but offers a standardized commodity with transparent pricing and several available buyers, choose a carefully priced barter or counterpurchase arrangement. If the proposed goods require processing, special permits, or a single buyer, demand more cash or reject the structure. If the transaction involves a plant, infrastructure, or future production, consider a buyback only after technical, legal, and market teams approve the long exposure.

Use this decision flow:

- If the buyer can fund the transaction in hard currency, choose cash. - If the buyer can provide part cash and a marketable commodity, choose counterpurchase. - If the goods have a public price, stable quality, and several likely buyers, consider direct barter. - If the goods require years of production or depend on a new facility, use buyback only with strong guarantees. - If the goods lack a reliable market, require cash, a bank-backed payment instrument, or a different buyer.

Mina's review would also separate **commercial value** from **contract value**. Suppose a buyer offers copper worth $100,000 at a recognized market price. After inspection, inland transport, export fees, insurance, financing, and a broker's commission, the seller may realize only $86,000. The contract should not credit the copper at $100,000 unless the buyer accepts responsibility for those costs or provides additional value. A realistic countertrade price must reflect what the seller can actually convert into money.

The agreement should also address default in both directions. If the buyer fails to deliver the reciprocal goods, the seller needs a cash claim, interest, and a right to suspend further performance. If the seller rejects conforming goods without a valid reason, the buyer needs a remedy. Countertrade remains trade, not a favor; each obligation requires measurable performance.

Making the Contractual Barter Engine Work

1. **Map the currency problem before proposing an exchange.** Confirm why the buyer lacks hard currency. A temporary banking delay requires a different solution from permanent capital controls. Ask for the permitted currencies, transfer limits, approval process, and expected payment dates. Record whether the buyer can pay a deposit, fund freight, or provide a bank guarantee. This information determines how much exposure the seller can safely accept.

2. **Define the original sale in ordinary commercial terms.** State the product, quantity, specifications, delivery point, inspection process, warranty, and cash price. Do not bury the main sale inside a vague reciprocal-trade promise. If the seller supplies 100 industrial pumps, the contract should identify the model, performance standard, packaging, delivery schedule, and acceptance test. A precise original sale gives the parties a reference point when they calculate the reciprocal obligation.

3. **Select reciprocal goods with an existing market.** Require samples, technical specifications, certificates of origin, and recent inspection records. Check whether the goods face import restrictions, quotas, sanctions, labeling rules, or special licensing requirements in the seller's country. Confirm at least two plausible buyers before accepting the goods. Two potential buyers matter because a single buyer can force a distressed sale and erase the expected margin.

4. **Calculate net realizable value.** Start with a defensible market price, then subtract inspection, storage, inland transport, ocean freight, insurance, customs charges, financing, brokerage, processing, and expected waste. For example, if the reciprocal goods carry a gross market value of $120,000 and total conversion costs reach $18,000, credit the goods at no more than $102,000 unless the contract assigns some costs to the other party. Add a quality discount when the specifications remain uncertain.

5. **Write an objective valuation formula.** Use a named price source, a stated quotation period, a currency, a delivery location, and an adjustment for grade. For a commodity, the formula might use the average published price during the five business days before shipment, adjusted for purity and freight. Avoid "prevailing market price" without identifying who determines it and what evidence that person

must use. Ambiguous pricing turns a commercial disagreement into a negotiation after the goods arrive.

6. **Assign delivery and risk at each transfer point.** State who arranges export clearance, import clearance, transport, insurance, inspection, and storage. Identify when title and risk move from one party to the other. Use the current version of the relevant **International Commercial Terms (Incoterms)** rule when appropriate, but write the practical responsibilities in the contract as well. A term alone cannot solve a mismatch between the contract and the parties' actual shipping process.

7. **Control quality before shipment, not after arrival.** Appoint an independent inspector and specify the testing method, sample size, inspection location, and deadline for objections. Require the seller of reciprocal goods to replace nonconforming goods or pay the shortfall in cash. If the goods can deteriorate, include shelf-life requirements and a rejection procedure. Quality disputes become expensive when the goods cross borders before either side verifies them.

8. **Protect against nonperformance.** Set deadlines for the main sale and the reciprocal purchase. Include a cash settlement amount if the buyer fails to deliver acceptable goods. Consider a bank guarantee, standby letter of credit, escrow, or parent-company guarantee when the exposure justifies the cost. The protection should cover the seller's actual replacement cost, not merely a symbolic penalty.

9. **Check compliance before signing.** Screen the parties, banks, vessels, brokers, end users, and goods against applicable sanctions and export-control rules. Review anti-bribery risks, especially when a government agency or politically connected intermediary participates. Confirm that customs authorities will accept the declared value and

that the proposed structure does not disguise a prohibited payment. A profitable transaction that violates trade controls creates losses no resale margin can repair.

10. **Build the resale plan before accepting inventory.** Name the broker, warehouse, processor, or end buyer responsible for converting the goods into cash. Obtain written indications of price and capacity rather than relying on informal interest. Set a maximum holding period. If the goods remain unsold after that period, trigger a price adjustment, cash settlement, or return right. Countertrade becomes manageable when the exit route exists before the entry obligation begins.

11. **Monitor the engine with a simple transaction file.** Track the original invoice value, reciprocal obligation, delivered quantity, accepted quantity, conversion costs, cash recovered, remaining exposure, and contract deadlines. Mina could review this file weekly while shipments remain open. A spreadsheet works if it records documents and owners; a trade-management system helps when the company handles many linked transactions. The purpose is not administrative complexity. The purpose is to detect a shortfall before it becomes an overdue claim.

12. **Close the transaction only after economic settlement.** Reconcile the goods received against the contract formula, record every cost, release guarantees only after final acceptance, and document any remaining cash balance. Compare the planned net value with the actual cash recovered. If a $100,000 reciprocal obligation produces only $82,000 after conversion costs, use that result when pricing the next deal. The Contractual Barter Engine improves through measured outcomes, not optimistic forecasts.

Act today:

- Identify one international customer whose currency restrictions affect payment. - List three goods that customer could provide and verify whether each has at least two potential buyers. - Calculate net realizable value after freight, inspection, taxes, storage, and brokerage. - Draft a payment schedule that requires partial cash and specifies a cash remedy for nonperformance. - Ask a trade lawyer, customs specialist, or experienced broker to review sanctions, import, and valuation risks before signing.

Countertrade succeeds when the parties exchange more than promises. They must exchange defined goods, defensible values, enforceable obligations, and a practical route back to liquidity. That discipline reveals the broader mechanics of markets: value depends not only on what an asset is worth on paper, but also on who can accept it, move it, and turn it into usable purchasing power.

CHAPTER 16

Time Banks and Peer-to-Peer Exchange

Why Time and Local Exchange Matter

What would your work be worth if the unit of account were an hour rather than a dollar? Time banks answer that question by recording services through time credits: one hour of tutoring earns one hour of help with bookkeeping, transport, repairs, or another approved service. Local barter networks use a related idea but may price exchanges in dollars, credits, goods, or negotiated combinations. Both systems turn reciprocity into a visible, organized market.

These systems matter because money does not measure every useful contribution equally. A retired electrician, a child-care provider, and a community organizer may lack spare cash but possess valuable skills. A time bank makes those skills exchangeable without requiring a direct "double coincidence of wants." Jonah, a 31-year-old community builder, could earn one time credit by helping a neighborhood group plan an event, then spend that credit on bicycle repairs or language practice.

Time credits do not automatically equal market wages, and local barter does not eliminate taxes, liability, scheduling problems, or quality differences. Treat them as exchange tools, not magical substitutes for cash. The practical objective is to identify where reciprocity lowers costs, fills unused capacity, and strengthens local relationships without hiding the true economic value of your time.

Your Toolkit for a Reliable Reciprocity Network

- **A time-bank platform:** Use software such as Community Weaver or a comparable local platform to list offers, requests, balances, and completed exchanges. Check whether a nearby time bank already operates before creating a new account; membership often costs nothing or requires a small annual contribution.

- **A clear exchange unit:** Define one time credit as one hour of completed service. Record travel, materials, preparation, and specialist work separately so participants do not mistake donated supplies for free labor.

- **A member profile and verification process:** Require each participant to state skills, service limits, location, availability, and references where appropriate. A local coordinator can verify identity at low cost through an application, phone call, and basic code of conduct.

- **A service ledger:** Keep a simple spreadsheet or platform record showing date, service, hours, materials, requester, provider, and approval status. This costs little but prevents disputes over balances and incomplete work.

- **A rate and materials policy:** Decide whether members exchange only time or also reimburse cash expenses. For example, one hour of gardening may earn one credit, while plants, fuel, and disposal fees remain the requester's responsibility.

- **Safety and liability rules:** Set boundaries for electrical work, medical assistance, child care, transport, and home access. Obtain appropriate insurance advice and require licensed professionals to follow local rules; a time credit does not replace a permit or professional duty.

- **A local communication channel:** Use the platform's messaging system, a private group, or a monthly bulletin to match offers with requests. Keep personal contact details private until both parties agree to share them.

- **A cash comparison sheet:** Record what a similar service would cost in the local market. This lets you measure savings without pretending that a time credit has the same purchasing power as cash.

The Hours-to-Value Converter

1. **Choose one concrete exchange goal.** Write a target such as "earn four time credits this month by providing event-planning help" or "replace $80 of household spending through local barter." A specific target prevents the network from becoming an untracked social activity.

2. **Inventory your usable capacity.** List services you can deliver safely within the next 30 days. Jonah might offer two hours of meeting facilitation, three hours of volunteer scheduling, and one hour of basic website editing each week. Exclude skills that require licenses, tools, or insurance you do not possess.

3. **Separate labor from expenses.** For each offer, state the time credit and the cash cost. "Two time credits for garden labor; requester supplies compost and pays the $12 delivery fee" creates a workable agreement. Without this separation, participants may accept a service and later dispute who pays for materials.

4. **Set a service boundary.** Define what the offer includes and excludes. Jonah's event-planning service could include a 30-minute planning call, a written schedule, and volunteer assignments, but

exclude venue contracts and paid advertising. Boundaries protect both sides from scope expansion.

5. **Join or create a local exchange group.** Search for a time bank, tool library, neighborhood exchange, professional trade group, or cooperative in your area. Review its rules, dispute process, privacy practices, and treatment of unused balances before you commit.

6. **Complete your profile with evidence.** Add examples, qualifications, service area, and available times. A community builder can list previous event types, planning tools, and references from organizations that received the work. Specific evidence improves matching and reduces the need for repeated explanations.

7. **Start with a low-risk exchange.** Choose a service that takes no more than two hours and requires limited access to property or personal information. A first exchange should test punctuality, communication, quality, and recordkeeping before either party agrees to a larger commitment.

8. **Confirm the agreement in writing.** Record the service, number of credits, deadline, location, materials, cancellation terms, and payment method. Use one sentence for each item. Written terms matter because time-based systems often rely on goodwill, and goodwill does not resolve conflicting memories.

9. **Deliver the service and document completion.** Note the start and end time, work completed, materials used, and any unfinished items. If the task changes, pause and obtain agreement before adding work. Do not quietly convert a one-hour exchange into a three-hour obligation.

10. **Transfer credits immediately.** The provider records the hours only after the requester confirms completion. Jonah should receive two credits after the community group accepts the event schedule, not merely after he attends the first meeting. Immediate recording keeps the ledger accurate and makes future exchanges possible.

11. **Measure the cash alternative.** Record the local cash price for a comparable service, then calculate the difference between that price and your actual out-of-pocket cost. If a two-hour barter exchange avoids a $60 service bill but requires $15 in materials, the practical saving equals $45, not $60.

12. **Review your effective return.** Apply the Hours-to-Value Converter: divide cash saved or earned by total hours contributed, including preparation and travel. If Jonah spends four total hours preparing an event plan and avoids a $100 professional fee while paying $20 for software, his practical return equals $20 per hour. This figure helps him decide whether the exchange supports his financial goals.

13. **Check the balance every month.** A positive balance means you have provided more than you received; a negative balance means the reverse. Neither position proves success. A large positive balance may indicate that members cannot supply what you need, while a large negative balance may create pressure to provide services you cannot safely deliver.

14. **Resolve problems quickly.** Contact the other party within 48 hours when work falls short, materials differ, or a deadline slips. Propose a repair: finish the task, return part of the credit, or involve

the coordinator. Fast correction protects the network's trust better than silent dissatisfaction.

15. **Report taxable or regulated activity correctly.** Ask a qualified tax professional how local law treats barter income, time credits, business expenses, and donated services. Keep records even when no cash changes hands. A reciprocal exchange can still create reporting, licensing, employment, or consumer-protection obligations.

16. **Scale only after three clean exchanges.** Expand your offer, accept longer jobs, or coordinate group projects after you complete three exchanges without unresolved disputes. This sequence gives you evidence about demand, reliability, and your true time cost before you expose more of your schedule.

Quick Reference for Time-Based Exchange

Exchange unit: Use one hour for one time credit unless the network states another rule. Do not assign different credit values to people based on occupation; that would turn a time bank into a wage market.

Cash comparison: Track the local cash price and your actual expenses. Practical value equals avoided or earned cash minus materials, travel, fees, and other direct costs.

Hours-to-Value Converter: Divide practical cash value by total hours, including planning and travel. If the result falls below your minimum acceptable return, renegotiate the scope or decline.

Materials rule: State who pays for supplies before work begins. Time credits cover labor only unless the written agreement says otherwise.

First exchange: Keep it to two hours or less and choose a low-risk task. Use the first exchange to test reliability, not to solve a major project.

Scope rule: Write what the service includes and excludes. If the requester adds work, pause and agree on extra credits or cash before continuing.

Balance check: Review credits monthly. If you hold many unused credits, request services or improve the network's matching process; if you owe many credits, schedule a realistic way to contribute.

Safety rule: Never use time credits to bypass licensing, insurance, permits, or professional standards. Decline work that creates legal or physical risk.

If demand exceeds supply: Offer a service that solves a repeated local problem, such as transport coordination, bookkeeping, translation, or home maintenance. Clear demand makes credits useful.

If supply exceeds demand: Narrow your offer, improve your profile, or ask members what they need before contributing more hours. More credits do not create wealth when the network cannot provide useful services in return.

If quality disappoints: Document the gap, request a correction, and use the dispute process. Do not retaliate through public accusations before the network reviews the facts.

If cash savings remain small: Keep the exchange only if it provides another measurable benefit, such as access to scarce skills, stronger local relationships, or reduced idle time. Otherwise, redirect those hours toward paid work, training, or a service with clearer value.

Time banks and local barter work best when participants treat reciprocity as an accountable economic arrangement. The ledger records trust, the agreement controls risk, and the Hours-to-Value Converter reveals whether goodwill also produces practical financial value. That discipline turns community exchange from an informal favor system into a small but measurable market.

CHAPTER 17

Money's Three Jobs: Medium, Unit, Store

Why Money's Three Jobs Matter

A single dollar can buy lunch today, price a used van tomorrow, and sit in a savings account for six months. Those actions look similar because they use the same object, but they depend on three different jobs: money acts as a **medium of exchange**, a **unit of account**, and a **store of value**. A currency can perform one job well while failing at another.

That distinction matters whenever prices rise, currencies weaken, credit freezes, or an asset market becomes difficult to trade. A business may accept dollars for a repair, quote the repair in dollars, and still move excess cash into inventory or short-term government securities because cash may lose purchasing power. Treating all three jobs as one creates poor decisions: a reliable payment method may not preserve wealth, and a stable measuring stick may not remain convenient for trade.

The Three-Role Stress Test gives you a practical way to separate these risks. After applying it, you can identify which money function you need, test whether your currency or asset performs that function, and choose a response that fits the problem instead of reacting to every monetary concern with the same solution.

The Three-Role Stress Test

The **medium of exchange** role answers a practical question: can people use money to settle transactions? A currency works as a medium when sellers accept it, buyers can transfer it, and payment systems complete transactions with reasonable speed and reliability. Cash, bank transfers, payment cards, and digital wallets can all perform this role. Barter struggles here because each trade requires a matching need. A plumber who wants fuel must find a fuel seller willing to accept plumbing work at an acceptable value and time.

The **unit of account** role answers a different question: can people quote, compare, record, and settle prices using the same measuring stick? A gym may charge $80 per month, pay a cleaner $22 per hour, and compare rent, equipment, and payroll in dollars. The dollar makes those costs comparable even when no transaction occurs between the gym and the equipment supplier. Inflation can damage this role by making old prices less informative. If a machine cost $4,000 last year and $4,800 today, the number alone does not tell you whether the machine became more valuable or the currency bought less.

The **store of value** role asks whether money can preserve purchasing power across time. A store of value does not need to maintain an identical price in every market. It needs to remain useful for future claims on goods and services. A checking-account balance may provide excellent payment access but weak long-term protection against rising prices. A productive business, diversified investments, or inflation-linked assets may preserve value better, but each carries market, business, liquidity, or legal risk.

Apply the Three-Role Stress Test in this order:

1. **Name the job.** Decide whether you need to pay, measure, or preserve purchasing power. This prevents you from using a long-term

asset as emergency cash or judging a payment system by its investment return. 2. **Test performance.** Check acceptance, price clarity, and purchasing power separately. A currency passes one test only when it performs that specific job under the conditions you face. 3. **Measure the failure cost.** Ask what happens if the role breaks for one day, one month, or one year. A delayed payment may create a late fee; a distorted unit of account may produce bad pricing; lost purchasing power may permanently reduce future choices. 4. **Match the remedy to the failure.** Keep liquid money for near-term obligations, use a consistent currency for records and prices, and select suitable assets for longer-term purchasing power. Do not expect one holding to solve every problem.

This framework also explains why historical money systems combined several instruments. Communities used credit records to track obligations, commodities or coins for settlement, and stored goods for future consumption. Barter could complete a specific exchange, but it did not automatically provide a common price measure or a dependable way to carry wealth forward.

Putting It Into Practice

Aisha, a 40-year-old personal finance coach, reviews her household and business finances after noticing that her monthly expenses have become harder to forecast. Her coaching practice receives client payments in dollars, records fees and expenses in dollars, and keeps its reserve in a dollar bank account. She does not assume that this arrangement gives every dollar the same economic function.

She applies the test to a six-month operating reserve of $18,000. Her immediate need involves the medium-of-exchange role: rent, software, taxes, and contractor invoices require accepted payment. Her next need involves the unit-of-account role: she must quote coaching packages and compare expenses without changing the measuring stick every week. Her final need involves the store-of-value role: money not required for six months should retain enough purchasing power to support future operations.

Aisha works through the decision as follows:

1. **List the timing of each obligation.** She identifies $3,000 due within 30 days, $4,500 due during months two and three, and $2,500 of expected tax payments during month six. She keeps $10,000 readily available because payment access matters more than investment return for these obligations. 2. **Separate pricing from payment.** She keeps all client contracts, invoices, and expense records in dollars. She does not switch prices to gold, foreign currency, or a digital token merely because those assets may hold value differently. A common unit keeps her revenue and costs comparable. 3. **Test the reserve's purchasing power.** She compares the cost of her recurring business basket - rent, software, insurance, and contractor hours - with the same basket six months earlier. If the basket costs more, the dollar reserve has lost purchasing power against her actual expenses, even though the account balance remains $18,000. 4. **Assign the remaining $8,000 by time and risk.** She places money needed within six months in a low-volatility, accessible vehicle and considers diversified long-term assets only for money she can leave invested. She avoids using a volatile asset for payroll because a market decline at the wrong time could force a sale. 5. **Review monthly.** On the first business day of each month, she checks the reserve balance, the next 90 days of bills, and the cost of her recurring business basket. The review shows whether the payment role, measurement role, and store-of-value role still work.

The expected outcome is not a perfect hedge against every monetary problem. Aisha gains something more useful: clarity about which risk she accepts. She preserves payment capacity, keeps records consistent, and avoids confusing a liquid balance with guaranteed wealth preservation.

Quick checklist

- Identify whether each dollar must pay, measure, or preserve value. - Keep near-term bills in an accepted and accessible form of money. - Use one clear unit for contracts, bookkeeping, and price comparisons. - Compare purchasing power against your actual household or business expense basket. - Keep volatile assets away from obligations that cannot wait. - Review the three roles when prices, payment access, or market conditions change.

What to Watch For

Mistaking payment access for wealth preservation

A bank balance can remain unchanged while the goods and services it buys become more expensive. That balance may perform the medium-of-exchange role perfectly and still perform the store-of-value role poorly.

Do this: Match the holding period to the purpose. Keep emergency and near-term spending money accessible, then evaluate longer-term assets for money you do not need soon.

Not this: Treat every dollar in a checking account as equally suitable for a three-year goal.

Using a stable price label to hide unstable purchasing power

A business can continue quoting prices in dollars while its costs change rapidly. The unit of account still functions operationally, but old price records may no longer guide profitable decisions.

Do this: Track the prices of the specific inputs that matter - rent, fuel, materials, labor, insurance, or software - and update quotes when those costs change.

Not this: Assume that a familiar number, such as last year's $1,000 project price, remains economically equivalent today.

Choosing a store of value that cannot meet a payment deadline

Gold, shares, property, and digital assets may serve long-term wealth goals, but their prices can move, and selling them can take time or create taxes and transaction costs. An asset that preserves value over a long period may still fail as a medium of exchange during tomorrow's payroll run.

Do this: Build a payment reserve before allocating surplus money to assets with price or liquidity risk.

Not this: Sell a long-term holding under pressure because you placed next month's bills in an asset designed for a different job.

Money works best when you judge each role on its own terms. A payment method must settle transactions, a unit of account must support clear comparison, and a store of value must protect future purchasing power well enough for its purpose. Once you separate those tests, currency and asset decisions become less theatrical and more mechanical - the same discipline that turns barter, markets, and modern money into systems you can evaluate rather than merely trust.

CHAPTER 18

Money as Servant, Not Master

The Stewardship Hierarchy: Giving Money Its Proper Place

"Money is a good servant but a bad master." The proverb becomes useful only when it changes a decision made at a kitchen table, in a brokerage account, or during a business expansion. Money should carry out a purpose. It should not quietly become the purpose.

Modern currency makes that discipline harder. A bank balance looks precise, liquid, and immediately available, while life goals often remain broad: security, freedom from unwanted work, education, health, family support, or meaningful projects. Without explicit rules, available cash begins to dictate behavior. A rising account balance can encourage unnecessary risk; a market decline can force a useful investment to sell at the wrong time; a high income can conceal uncontrolled commitments.

Key insight: Money serves life goals only when each dollar receives a job before emotion, advertising, or market noise assigns one.

The Stewardship Hierarchy provides that order. It places obligations and resilience before growth, and growth before speculation. The hierarchy does not require extreme frugality or avoidance of risk. It requires a clear sequence: protect the person and household, preserve flexibility, fund defined goals, then accept measured uncertainty for goals that can tolerate loss.

For Martin, a 48-year-old physician, the distinction matters. His income supports a large mortgage, private-school expenses, retirement contributions, and professional obligations. A portfolio can appear healthy while his financial structure remains fragile if one serious illness, career change, or market decline would force him to sell assets or borrow at the wrong time. Stewardship turns that concern into operating rules.

Core Principles of the Stewardship Hierarchy

1. Protect the foundation before pursuing growth.

The foundation includes essential living costs, insurance, taxes, high-cost debt, and cash reserves. These items come first because a household cannot treat invested assets as long-term capital when it may need them next month. A stock portfolio may offer attractive future returns, but it cannot guarantee a favorable selling date.

Martin begins by calculating his household's essential monthly cost rather than using total spending. His mortgage, utilities, food, insurance, transportation, and required professional expenses total $18,000 per month. He sets a reserve target of nine months, or $162,000, because his income depends partly on clinical work and his household carries substantial fixed commitments.

This reserve does not need to earn the highest possible return. Its job is to prevent forced decisions. Martin keeps it in insured deposit accounts and short-term government securities that match his need for access. He also reviews disability, life, liability, and property coverage. Insurance transfers a large financial loss when self-funding that loss would damage his goals.

2. Convert values into dated, funded goals.

A vague goal cannot produce a reliable money rule. "Retire comfortably" does not identify a contribution, an investment mix, or a deadline. A useful goal names the amount, date, and consequence of falling short.

Martin separates his goals into three time ranges. He wants $120,000 for a home renovation in three years, continued retirement funding beginning at age 60, and a flexible fund for supporting family members or reducing clinical work. He does not place all three goals in the same investment account because they face different time risks.

A goal within three years receives protection from large market swings. A retirement goal with a twelve-year horizon can accept more fluctuation, provided Martin can continue working or adjust spending if markets fall. The reason for separating accounts rests on purchasing power and timing: a temporary decline matters little to money needed in twelve years, but it matters greatly to money needed for a contractor's deposit next spring.

3. Use a decision rule before a feeling.

A decision rule states what action follows a known condition. It prevents a temporary emotion from becoming a permanent financial mistake.

Martin writes: "I will not use retirement assets for a renovation." He adds: "I will invest the renovation fund only in assets whose value I can tolerate seeing decline modestly without delaying the project." For his investment portfolio, he sets a review rule: rebalance when an asset class moves materially away from its planned range, rather than buying or selling because a headline creates fear.

Rules work because markets and personal finances create pressure at different times. During a market decline, Martin may feel that selling protects him. His written rule reminds him that the retirement account funds a distant goal and that his reserve covers near-term needs. During a market surge, the same rule prevents him from treating recent gains as proof that he should take a much larger risk.

4. Measure money by service, not status.

A dollar has no success of its own. It succeeds when it performs its assigned job at an acceptable cost and risk. A larger portfolio may represent progress, but it may also reflect money trapped in an unsuitable account, excessive concentration, or spending that produces little value.

Martin reviews each major account with three questions: Which goal does it serve? When will he need the money? What loss or restriction can he accept? If an account has no clear answer, he redirects it, spends it intentionally, or removes it from the portfolio.

This principle also changes how Martin evaluates income. A $40,000 increase in annual earnings does not automatically justify a $40,000 increase in recurring expenses. He directs the increase first toward reserves, debt reduction, and defined goals. Only the remainder supports lifestyle expansion. Money remains a servant when higher income buys more control rather than more obligations.

A Practical Walkthrough: Martin's Annual Money Rules

Martin uses the following process every January and after any major change in income, health, family needs, or debt.

1. **List the household's fixed obligations.** Martin records mortgage payments of $7,200 per month, essential household

spending of $7,000, insurance and professional costs of $2,300, and required debt payments of $1,500. His essential total equals $18,000 per month. He excludes travel, luxury purchases, and optional subscriptions because those expenses can stop during a financial shock.

2. **Set the foundation target.** Nine months of essential costs produces a reserve target of $162,000. Martin currently holds $105,000, so he directs $4,750 per month toward the reserve until he adds the missing $57,000. At that pace, he reaches the target in twelve months. The calculation gives his cash a specific assignment instead of allowing it to drift between checking and investments.

3. **Separate goals by date.** Martin lists the renovation at $120,000 due in three years. He contributes $3,333 per month before considering any investment return. This approach avoids depending on market gains to meet a fixed bill. He places the money in short-term, lower-volatility holdings suited to the deadline.

4. **Fund long-term growth.** After the reserve contribution and renovation funding, Martin directs $9,000 per month toward retirement accounts and a taxable investment account. He chooses a diversified mix based on his twelve-year horizon and ability to continue working. Diversification spreads exposure across different assets; it does not remove risk, but it reduces dependence on one company, sector, or market.

5. **Write the spending rule.** Martin allows lifestyle spending to rise only after the foundation target remains full and the renovation contribution stays on schedule. He sets a $12,000 annual discretionary budget for travel and major purchases. He can spend it freely within

that limit because the money already has a defined place in the hierarchy.

6. **Create an investment review rule.** Martin reviews accounts quarterly but makes changes only when a goal, time horizon, or planned allocation changes. He rebalances annually or when an investment category moves far enough from its target to alter the portfolio's risk. He does not trade in response to daily price movements.

The structure produces a visible difference:

Area	Before the rules	After the rules
Cash reserve	$105,000 with no target	$162,000 target, funded over 12 months
Renovation money	Mixed with investment assets	$3,333 monthly contribution
Retirement funding	Variable after spending	$9,000 monthly contribution
Lifestyle increases	Based on income and mood	Allowed after priority funding
Market decisions	Headline-driven	Governed by written conditions

Martin should measure success after twelve months using practical tests. Did the reserve reach its target? Did the renovation account remain on schedule? Did retirement contributions continue during market volatility? Did recurring expenses rise faster than income? These answers reveal whether money served the plan. A portfolio statement alone cannot answer them.

Troubleshooting the Hierarchy Under Pressure

Problem: Martin keeps investing while carrying expensive debt and an incomplete reserve.

Why it happens: Investment growth feels productive, while debt repayment and cash reserves appear inactive. Martin may also focus on the tax advantages of an account without considering the cost of borrowing elsewhere. If a credit balance charges a high rate, the household accepts a known cost while hoping for an uncertain investment return.

Fix: Martin lists every debt, its interest rate, minimum payment, and repayment date. He maintains enough cash for immediate obligations, captures any available employer retirement contribution, and then directs additional money toward the highest-cost debt before increasing optional investing. This sequence protects flexibility and removes a guaranteed drag from his finances. He reviews the arrangement after the debt falls and redirects the freed payment toward long-term goals.

Problem: A market decline causes Martin to abandon a long-term plan.

Why it happens: Martin sees a lower account value and interprets it as a permanent loss, even though the retirement goal remains years away. News coverage compresses the time horizon into a single frightening day. The emotional pressure becomes strongest when the portfolio contains money that Martin does not actually need immediately.

Fix: Martin checks the hierarchy before changing investments. He confirms that the reserve remains intact, the renovation fund matches its deadline, and current income covers essential costs. If those conditions hold, he leaves the long-term allocation in place and continues scheduled contributions. If a decline exposes a genuine mismatch - such as too much risk for a goal approaching within three years - he reduces risk for that goal specifically rather than selling everything.

Problem: Martin earns more but feels no greater control.

Why it happens: Higher income often expands recurring commitments before it strengthens the balance sheet. A larger home, additional staff, expensive memberships, and financed purchases can turn a temporary income increase into permanent obligations. Money then serves consumption first, while the stated goals receive whatever remains.

Fix: Martin divides every increase in after-tax income before spending it. He assigns a fixed amount to the reserve or debt, a fixed amount to long-term goals, and a defined remainder to lifestyle. For example, from an additional $5,000 per month, he may direct $2,000 to retirement, $1,500 to debt reduction, $1,000 to the renovation, and $500 to discretionary spending. He reviews the split after three months, not after one unusually profitable month. This preserves the benefit of higher earnings without allowing temporary income to create permanent pressure.

The Stewardship Hierarchy does not ask Martin to reject money, ambition, or risk. It asks him to place each one in the correct order. Cash protects choices, investments fund distant aims, and spending expresses values. When written rules govern those functions, money becomes measurable and useful rather than commanding. The broader mechanics of markets matter greatly, but they serve the household best when the household decides first what money must accomplish.

CHAPTER 19

Behavioral Finance: The Bias Inventory

Setting the Stage: Why Biases Belong on the Trading Checklist

Tessa, 35, opens her brokerage account after seeing a stock rise from $42 to $58 in three weeks. She feels late, so she buys 40 shares at $58. The price falls to $51 the next day. Instead of reviewing the company, she tells herself the market has mispriced it and buys 40 more shares. At $44, she refuses to sell because doing so would "lock in" the loss. One decision now contains several predictable distortions: chasing recent performance, treating the purchase price as meaningful, and defending an earlier judgment.

Biases do not require carelessness or low intelligence. They arise because the mind uses shortcuts when information arrives quickly, uncertainty remains high, and money creates emotional pressure. Trading makes those conditions worse. Prices move before you can verify every fact, headlines reward urgency, and a position can make neutral analysis feel personally threatening.

You need only three materials to begin: a written investment policy, a transaction log, and a calculator or spreadsheet. Your log should record the date, asset, price, position size, reason for entry, invalidation point, and exit rule. Without those records, you will remember the decision selectively and mistake a favorable outcome for a sound process.

The goal does not involve eliminating bias. You cannot remove every shortcut from judgment. The practical goal involves detecting the bias before it changes position size, entry price, holding period, or risk tolerance.

The Bias Radar: A Practical Map of Distorted Decisions

The Bias Radar places each proposed trade under four questions: What information am I noticing? What am I refusing to notice? What emotion is pushing the timing? What rule would I follow if I had no position?

This structure turns a vague feeling into an inspection. Use it before entering, adding to, holding, or selling a position. The sequence matters because bias often appears as a change in action rather than a false statement.

1. **Record the trigger.** Write the exact event that attracted your attention. "The stock rose 38% in three weeks" differs from "the business increased cash flow." The first describes price movement; the second describes an operating fact.

2. **Separate facts from interpretation.** Create two columns. In the fact column, record information that another person could verify, such as revenue, debt, cash balance, guidance, or price. In the interpretation column, write conclusions such as "the market is waking up" or "this dip is a buying opportunity." This separation exposes confirmation bias, the tendency to favor evidence that supports an existing view.

3. **Name the active bias.** Use plain labels. Common entries include: - **Recency bias:** giving recent events too much weight. - **Anchoring:** treating a past price, forecast, or purchase cost as a

reference point without a current reason. - **Loss aversion:** resisting a necessary sale because the loss feels more painful than an equivalent gain feels satisfying. - **Confirmation bias:** searching for support while dismissing contrary evidence. - **Herding:** copying a crowd because agreement feels safer. - **Overconfidence:** assigning too much reliability to your forecast or skill. - **Disposition effect:** selling winners too quickly while holding losers too long. - **Sunk-cost thinking:** defending a decision because you already spent money or effort on it.

4. **Run the counterfactual test.** Ask, "If I held cash today, would I buy this position at this price?" If the answer is no, the existing position may control the decision. Ask a second question: "What evidence would make me change my mind?" If you cannot name evidence, confirmation bias has likely replaced analysis.

5. **Apply a written rule.** Set the position size, review date, and invalidation condition before acting. An invalidation condition states what would disprove the original thesis. For example, "I will review the position if gross margin falls below 35% for two reporting periods" creates a measurable trigger. "I will sell if things look bad" creates an emotional argument at the worst moment.

Consider Tessa's position. She bought 40 shares at $58, spending $2,320. At $44, the position is worth $1,760, a $560 unrealized loss. Her original thesis involved a new product expected to improve sales. The company later delayed that product by two quarters, while debt increased from $80 million to $105 million. The relevant evidence now contradicts the thesis. Her purchase price of $58 does not predict the stock's value; it only anchors her emotions.

The Bias Radar produces a different decision. Tessa writes: "If I held cash, I would not buy this stock at $44 because the product delay and higher debt weaken the original case." She sells the 80 shares and limits the loss to $1,120 from the full position. The sale does not prove that the company cannot recover. It proves that she followed an invalidation rule instead of defending an old price.

The same tool catches bullish distortions. Suppose Tessa sees a popular technology fund rise from $100 to $112 and reads only favorable commentary. She plans to invest $6,000 because "everyone is positioned for the next move." The Radar asks her to compare the fund's current holdings, fees, concentration, and valuation with her existing portfolio. If the purchase would raise her exposure to the same sector from $9,000 to $15,000, her enthusiasm may conceal concentration risk. A 40% decline in that sector would reduce the combined exposure by $6,000 before considering the rest of her portfolio. The number makes the hidden risk visible.

Try It Yourself: A Fifteen-Minute Bias Audit

Use the Bias Radar on one real position or one trade you are considering. Choose a position large enough to matter but not so complex that several unrelated decisions become mixed together. Tessa's delayed-product stock works as a model; your own holding should include a current price, a written reason for ownership, and at least one available business or market fact.

Prepare a sheet with these columns:

Question	Your entry
What changed today?	
What facts support the decision?	
What facts oppose it?	
Which bias may be active?	
What would I do with cash instead?	
What condition invalidates the thesis?	
What action follows?	

Set a timer for 15 minutes. For the first three minutes, write the trigger without checking commentary or social media. For the next five minutes, enter three supporting facts and three opposing facts. If you cannot find three opposing facts, do not treat that absence as proof of safety; search the company filing, fund report, or market data directly.

Spend the next three minutes naming the bias. Use one primary label and, if necessary, one secondary label. Tessa's entry might read: "Primary: anchoring to $58. Secondary: loss aversion." Then answer the cash question. If the answer differs from your current action, write why. Finally, set one measurable rule and one review date.

Suppose you hold 25 shares purchased at $120, now priced at $96. You originally expected earnings growth, but the latest report shows falling sales and reduced guidance. You would not buy at $96 if you held cash. Your rule says, "Sell if guidance falls and the growth thesis no longer holds." The expected outcome is a sale of 25 shares for $2,400, compared with the $3,000 purchase cost, and a documented decision based on changed facts rather than the desire to recover $600.

Do not judge the audit by whether the price rises after you sell. Judge it by whether your action matched the rule and whether the record would make sense six months later. A good completion check includes:

- One named bias. - Three supporting and three opposing facts. - One cash comparison. - One measurable invalidation rule. - One recorded action and review date.

Common Pitfalls in Bias Detection

Mistaking a good outcome for a good decision

A biased trade can make money. A disciplined trade can lose money. Short-term outcomes therefore provide weak evidence about decision quality. Tessa might buy a crowded stock from $58 and watch it reach $70, even though her only reason involved recent price strength. The gain would reward the process by accident and make the same mistake more likely later.

Do this: Score the decision by process: evidence recorded, opposing facts considered, position size controlled, and exit rule defined.

Not this: Keep using a weak method because one trade produced a profit.

Treating the purchase price as a market fact

The price you paid matters for taxes and personal accounting, but it does not establish current value. Anchoring becomes especially strong when a position falls below its entry price. Tessa's $58 purchase tells her where she acted, not what the stock should be worth today.

Do this: Revalue the asset from current earnings, cash flows, balance-sheet strength, valuation, and risk. Ask whether you would buy it today with cash.

Not this: Hold until the asset returns to your entry price merely to feel even.

Searching for a label instead of changing the decision

Naming confirmation bias does not stop confirmation bias. Some investors identify the bias, then continue reading only bullish commentary and increase the position anyway. The label has value only when it changes a rule, size, timing, or review process.

Do this: Require three opposing facts and write the condition that would invalidate the thesis. Reduce or delay the position when you cannot answer clearly.

Not this: Treat self-awareness as protection while leaving the trade unchanged.

A bias inventory works best when you complete it before urgency takes control. Prices, headlines, and crowds will continue to supply pressure; the written Radar gives that pressure a visible shape. Once you can see the shortcut, you can decide whether it belongs in the trade - or whether it should stay outside your portfolio.

CHAPTER 20

Overconfidence and Too-Much Trading

What Overconfidence Costs

Brandon was 26 when he began day trading from a laptop beside his regular workbench. A profitable morning convinced him that he had found a repeatable edge. By Friday, he had opened and closed dozens of positions, paid a commission or spread on every trade, and ended the week with less money than he started with. His losing trades did not result from one dramatic market collapse. They came from repeated small decisions made with more confidence than evidence.

Overconfidence means assigning too much weight to your own judgment, skill, or forecast. In markets, it often appears after a short run of success. A trader mistakes favorable conditions for personal ability, increases position size, trades more often, and treats contrary information as a temporary obstacle. The danger does not depend on intelligence. A capable person can understand markets well and still overestimate how accurately they can predict the next price move.

Churn means buying and selling so frequently that activity itself becomes a major source of cost. Each transaction can create a spread, commission, platform charge, tax consequence, or execution loss. A trade does not need to lose sharply to damage wealth. If the expected advantage remains small while costs arrive with certainty, repeated trading can convert a modest edge into a negative result.

The **Skill-Confidence Gap** measures the distance between what your results justify and what your confidence assumes. Confidence can rise after three successful trades, while actual skill requires a much larger and more varied record. The gap becomes dangerous when confidence controls trade size, frequency, or risk before evidence supports those decisions. Barter offers a useful comparison: a direct exchange works only when both parties value the goods accurately enough to agree. Market trading adds a further problem - prices move while you negotiate, and every mistake carries a monetary cost.

How the Skill-Confidence Gap Creates Churn

Overconfidence usually develops through a chain of understandable decisions. First, a trader experiences a favorable outcome. The outcome may come from a sound process, but it may also reflect a broad market rise, a lucky entry, or a temporary price pattern. The trader then explains the result as proof of superior reading or timing. That explanation changes behavior: the trader watches more closely, acts more quickly, and trusts personal judgment more than a written rule.

The next step involves **attribution error**, the tendency to credit skill for favorable results while blaming outside conditions for unfavorable results. Brandon recorded his winning trades as evidence that he could read momentum. He described losing trades as bad news, market manipulation, or poor liquidity. That interpretation protected his confidence, but it prevented learning. If every win confirms skill and every loss receives an external explanation, the record cannot correct the belief.

Trading frequency then rises. A trader who believes that skill creates profit begins searching for opportunities constantly. A quiet market feels like an invitation to find an overlooked move rather than a reason to wait. Brandon shifted from trading only after a clear setup to trading small price movements throughout the day. The more he traded, the more decisions he made under time pressure. His attention narrowed to entry points and recent price action, while costs accumulated in the background.

The arithmetic remains simple. Suppose a trader makes 20 round trips in a week and loses an average of $8 through the spread and execution on each completed trade. The market must produce $160 in gross advantage before the account reaches its starting point. If the trader increases activity to 60 round trips, the required advantage rises to $480. A trader can feel active, informed, and disciplined while spending more on transactions than the strategy earns.

The Skill-Confidence Gap also changes risk. A trader who expects a high probability of being right may hold a losing position longer, add to it, or reject a stop-loss rule. The trader does not view the action as a new risk; the trader views it as a temporary delay before the original judgment proves correct. That reasoning confuses conviction with information. A market price does not become more likely to reverse because someone has already lost money on the position.

Use a written control process before confidence reaches the trading screen:

1. Record the reason for every trade before placing it. State the entry condition, expected holding period, exit rule, maximum loss, and estimated transaction cost. 2. Record the result after closing the position. Separate market movement, execution quality, fees, and the outcome of the original idea. 3. Review trades on a fixed schedule, such as every Friday evening. Do not revise the rules after one result. Look

for repeated behavior across at least several weeks. 4. Set a trading-frequency limit in advance. When you reach the limit, stop for the session even if another setup appears. 5. Reduce position size whenever your actual record no longer supports your confidence.

This process works because it separates a good decision from a good outcome. A trade can lose money while following the rules, and a trade can make money while violating them. Without that separation, luck teaches the wrong lesson.

Applying the Skill-Confidence Gap to Day Trading

Brandon began with $12,000 and a simple momentum approach. He bought shares after a sharp upward move and sold when the price weakened. During his first week, four trades produced a total gain of $420 before costs. He concluded that fast reactions gave him an advantage. During the next three weeks, he increased his daily activity and began trading before his setup fully formed.

His account then showed a different pattern:

Measure	First week	Following three weeks
Completed round trips	8	74
Average holding time	3 hours	28 minutes
Gross trading result	$420	$310
Estimated spreads, fees, and execution loss	$96	$590
Result after trading costs	$324	-$280

The figures did not prove that momentum trading could never work. They showed that Brandon's behavior changed faster than his evidence justified. He had not demonstrated that he could predict short-term price movement after costs. He had demonstrated that one favorable week increased his confidence.

Brandon used the Skill-Confidence Gap to rebuild his process.

1. He defined one setup precisely: a price move followed by a specific consolidation pattern and a maximum entry price. He rejected trades that lacked those conditions. 2. He capped himself at three completed trades per day. The cap prevented boredom and frustration from creating new positions. 3. He risked a fixed dollar amount on each trade rather than increasing size after a win. He calculated the exit price before entering. 4. He added an estimated cost line to his trading log. The estimate included the bid-ask spread, commission, and expected slippage - the difference between the displayed price and the price he actually received. 5. He reviewed every trade at the end of the week and marked it as rule-following or rule-breaking before judging whether it made money. 6. He paused live trading for two weeks after three rule-breaking trades in one week. He used that period to review the log rather than trying to recover losses through more activity.

After four weeks, Brandon had fewer trades and a lower gross gain than during his most active period. His net result improved because costs fell and impulsive entries declined. More important, he could identify what his record actually supported. The evidence suggested that he handled a narrow setup with modest size; it did not support the belief that he could profit from every short-term movement.

The same test applies outside day trading. A small business owner who repeatedly changes suppliers after one price increase may believe constant switching demonstrates bargaining skill. The owner should calculate delivery delays, defective goods, staff time, and emergency purchases before claiming savings. An investor who sells one fund after a disappointing month may believe quick decisions protect capital. The investor should compare the sale with the original plan, the fund's stated role, and the cost of replacing it. In each case, activity can look like control while hidden costs reduce the result.

A favorable result does not establish a durable edge. A short winning run can reflect skill, luck, or conditions that no longer exist. Treat early success as a reason to collect better evidence, not as permission to increase size. Keep the original position size until your records show that the process works across different market conditions and after all costs.

Trading costs turn confidence into a measurable liability. Overconfidence matters financially because it increases the number of decisions that carry friction. Add spreads, fees, taxes where relevant, and slippage to every review. If the strategy needs frequent trading to produce a small expected gain, calculate whether the gain remains after those costs. A strategy that survives only before expenses has no usable edge.

The best defense against the Skill-Confidence Gap is a rule that limits behavior before emotion arrives. Set the maximum number of trades, maximum loss, position size, and review schedule while calm. Record the reason before entering and classify the decision afterward. These controls do not eliminate uncertainty; they stop confidence from silently expanding the risks you take.

Key actions: keep a pre-trade and post-trade log, calculate total costs, cap trading frequency, hold position size steady while gathering evidence, and judge decisions by rule-following rather than by isolated outcomes. Wealth grows when judgment improves faster than activity expands.

CHAPTER 21

Loss Aversion and the Disposition Effect

The Foundation: Why Losses Feel Larger Than Gains

What would you do if an investment fell 25 percent after you bought it: sell it, investigate it, or wait until it returned to your purchase price? Your answer may depend less on the investment's future than on the emotional meaning you attach to the loss. Many investors sell profitable assets quickly to "lock in" a win, while they keep declining assets because selling would make the loss feel final. That paired behavior creates a damaging pattern: winners leave the portfolio too soon, and losers consume capital for too long.

Economists call the first tendency the **disposition effect**. It describes the habit of realizing gains quickly and postponing losses. **Loss aversion** explains why this happens: a loss usually creates more psychological discomfort than an equal gain creates satisfaction. The purchase price becomes an emotional reference point. Once an asset trades below it, the investor starts waiting for a return to break even rather than asking whether the asset still deserves capital today.

The central correction is the **Loss-Proof Reframe**: stop judging an asset against your purchase price and judge it against the best use of your money now. Your original purchase price cannot change, and the market does not know what you paid. The relevant question is not, "Can this recover my loss?" It is, "If I had cash today, would I buy this asset at its current price?" If the answer is no, holding it requires a stronger reason than hope.

This framework does not mean selling every declining investment or holding every winner indefinitely. A sound investment can decline because markets move, while a weak investment can rise temporarily. The decision requires a defined thesis, a current valuation, and a rule for changing course. Without those elements, waiting becomes an emotional strategy disguised as patience.

Understanding the Process: How the Disposition Effect Takes Control

The pattern usually develops through a sequence.

1. **The purchase creates a reference point.** The investor records the entry price as the standard for success. A stock bought at $40 feels "safe" at $42 and "wrong" at $35, even when new information has changed its value.

2. **A gain triggers relief and fear.** At $48, the investor may sell because the gain feels real but fragile. Selling removes the fear that the profit could disappear. The investor receives emotional certainty instead of evaluating whether the asset could reasonably be worth more.

3. **A loss triggers denial and waiting.** At $32, selling would turn an unrealized loss into a visible result. The investor therefore searches for reasons to wait: a coming product launch, a market rebound, or a return to the old price. Each reason may sound analytical, but the hidden goal often remains break-even.

4. **Time increases attachment.** The longer the investor holds, the more effort goes into defending the original decision. This creates

a second trap: selling would not only recognize a loss but also admit that the original judgment failed.

5. **Opportunity cost disappears from view.** Capital tied to a weak asset cannot fund a stronger one. A $5,000 position that remains stagnant for two years may cause more damage through missed opportunities than through its visible price decline.

The Loss-Proof Reframe interrupts this sequence by separating three questions. First, what facts supported the original purchase? Second, which of those facts still hold? Third, what alternative could use the money better today? Write the answers before checking the current price. This order reduces the chance that the latest price movement will dictate the entire judgment.

Review each holding on a fixed schedule, such as the first weekend of every month. A fixed review prevents constant emotional checking, while a monthly interval gives the investment thesis enough time to develop. Review sooner when a major event changes the business, debt load, regulation, management, or competitive position.

For each holding, record four items: the current price, the original thesis, evidence that supports the thesis, and evidence that weakens it. Add a fifth item: the action you would take if you held cash instead. This final question exposes whether you still want the asset or merely want to avoid realizing the loss.

Use a sell rule that depends on facts rather than discomfort. For example, sell when the original thesis breaks, when the asset no longer fits your risk limit, or when another opportunity offers a clearly stronger use of the capital. Do not use "sell when the price returns to my purchase price" as the main rule. That rule treats an arbitrary historical number as if it carried economic meaning.

For winners, apply the same discipline in reverse. Ask whether the asset remains attractive at today's price. If it does, keep it despite the gain. If its valuation has become unreasonable or the thesis has weakened, sell despite the gain. The objective is not to maximize the number of winning trades. The objective is to improve the quality of capital allocation.

Applying the Loss-Proof Reframe: Keiko's Portfolio Review

Keiko, a 33-year-old project manager, built a $20,000 investment account from regular savings. She owned two exchange-traded funds and three individual stocks. One technology stock had fallen from $50 to $35, leaving her with a $1,500 paper loss on 100 shares. Another company had risen from $40 to $58, producing an $1,800 gain on the same number of shares.

Keiko wanted to keep the losing stock until it returned to $50. She also wanted to sell the winning stock because "a gain is a gain." That response showed the disposition effect clearly: she treated the losing position as unfinished business and the winning position as a completed success.

She used the Loss-Proof Reframe during her monthly review:

1. **Write the original thesis.** Keiko bought the declining stock because revenue had grown, debt appeared manageable, and management planned to expand into a new market. She bought the winning stock because it had strong cash generation and a broad customer base.

2. **Check current evidence.** The declining company had missed its sales target twice, increased borrowing, and delayed the expansion. The winning company had continued to grow sales, maintained its cash

position, and traded at a price she considered reasonable after comparing its earnings outlook with similar businesses.

3. **Apply the cash test.** Keiko asked, "If I had $3,500 in cash today, would I buy 100 shares of the declining stock at $35?" She answered no. She would not buy it without evidence that sales had stabilized and borrowing had stopped rising. She then asked whether she would buy the winning stock at $58. Her answer was yes, although she would buy fewer shares because the price had risen.

4. **Choose the action.** Keiko sold the declining position at $35 and moved the proceeds into a broad market fund rather than immediately selecting another individual stock. She kept the winning stock and set a review condition: sell if its valuation became unreasonable, its cash generation weakened materially, or its business thesis changed.

5. **Measure the result.** She recorded the sale price, the reason for selling, and the alternative investment. After three months, she compared the replacement fund with the old stock - not against the $50 purchase price, but against what her capital actually earned after the decision. She also reviewed whether the winning stock still met her written conditions.

This process did not guarantee a profit. It produced something more useful: a decision based on current evidence rather than emotional recovery. Keiko also avoided a common mistake - selling the winner automatically. The winning position remained in the account because its present prospects justified ownership, not because its past gain felt satisfying.

A practical review sheet can look like this:

Question	Declining stock	Winning stock
Current price	$35	$58
Original thesis still intact?	No; sales missed and debt increased	Yes; cash generation remains strong
Would I buy today?	No	Yes, at a controlled position size
Action	Sell and redirect capital	Hold and review monthly
Trigger for reconsideration	Evidence of stabilization	Valuation or business deterioration

Keiko's timeline also mattered. She completed the review on one date, placed the trade the next day, and scheduled the next review for one month later. She did not check the sold stock every hour to see whether it rebounded. That behavior would have restored the original emotional anchor and encouraged regret-driven decisions.

Avoiding Mistakes That Preserve Bad Decisions

Mistake: Waiting for the purchase price

The root cause is treating break-even as a financial objective. The market does not owe an asset a return to the price you paid. A company can deteriorate permanently while its former price remains psychologically powerful.

Do this: Rewrite every holding decision in current terms: "At today's price, the expected return and risk justify ownership," or "They do not." Sell when the thesis breaks, even if the position shows a loss.

Not this: "I will sell when it gets back to $50."

Mistake: Selling winners without checking future value

The root cause is confusing a realized gain with a completed investment. A gain does not prove that the asset has reached fair value. Selling solely to protect a profit can remove strong holdings while leaving weaker ones untouched.

Do this: Review profitable positions with the same cash test used for losing positions. Consider taxes, concentration, valuation, and your time horizon, then decide whether the asset remains worth owning.

Not this: "It went up, so I should take the money."

Mistake: Replacing analysis with a stop-loss number

The root cause is using a price movement as a substitute for understanding the asset. A fixed decline may protect capital in some situations, but it can also force a sale during ordinary volatility. Conversely, refusing to sell because the decline has not reached a chosen number can prolong a broken thesis.

Do this: Pair any price limit with a business or portfolio reason. Review debt, cash flow, competitive position, position size, and the original investment case. Use a written rule before emotions become intense.

Not this: "I will hold because it has only fallen 15 percent," or "I will sell automatically because it fell 10 percent," without checking what changed.

Quick reference: Ignore the purchase price when judging today's decision. Ask whether you would buy the asset now, identify the evidence that supports or breaks the thesis, compare the position with realistic alternatives, and apply the same standard to winners and losers. A loss becomes useful when it improves the allocation of your next dollar. That shift - from defending yesterday's choice to evaluating today's opportunity - connects personal investing with the wider mechanics of markets, where capital constantly moves toward its most valuable use.

CHAPTER 22

Anchoring to Prices and Narratives

The Price That Stayed After the Business Changed

A share price can remain psychologically powerful long after the facts that created it have disappeared. Graham, a 55-year-old chief financial officer, saw that problem when his company considered buying a regional supplier. The supplier's shares had traded near $42 for most of the previous year. After a temporary production failure, the price fell to $27. Six months later, production had returned to normal, but the company's earnings outlook had weakened permanently because a major customer had moved to a cheaper competitor.

The board still treated $42 as the "real" value. Graham heard the reference repeatedly: "We are buying at a discount to where the stock used to trade." That sentence sounded disciplined, but it smuggled an old price into a new decision. The supplier now faced lower future sales, higher financing costs, and a costly equipment replacement. Its earlier price did not measure those changed conditions.

The risk extended beyond the purchase price. Graham's company already held inventory from the same supplier, purchased when management expected demand to recover quickly. That inventory tied up cash and created another anchor. Managers resisted marking it down because the original cost appeared to prove its worth. Each decision then defended the previous decision: the supplier should be worth more because it once traded at $42, and the inventory should be worth more because the company once paid its original price.

At stake stood $18 million in cash, a potential acquisition, and the credibility of the finance team. If Graham accepted the old reference points, the company could overpay for a shrinking business while hiding losses in inventory. If he rejected them without a clear method, colleagues could dismiss his analysis as excessively cautious. He needed a process that separated current value from remembered value.

Graham's Anchor Reset Routine

Graham began by removing historical prices from the first page of the acquisition review. He asked the finance team to prepare three separate figures: the supplier's current market value, the value supported by its expected cash generation, and the replacement cost of its operating assets. The team used a five-year cash-flow forecast, recent customer commitments, debt terms, and the cost of replacing the supplier's equipment. They did not use the $42 share price in those calculations.

The result exposed the anchor. At $42, the supplier's total equity value implied strong sales recovery and stable profit margins. Yet the customer loss reduced expected annual revenue by $9 million, and the replacement equipment required $6 million in capital spending. Under the updated forecast, the company's cash generation supported a value closer to $29 per share. The old price did not become irrelevant because it was old; it became weak evidence because the business had changed.

Graham then required the team to write a "change list" before discussing the offer. Each item had to describe a fact that had changed since the reference price:

- the largest customer had left; - borrowing costs had increased; - equipment required replacement; - management had cut the sales forecast; - the supplier had lost bargaining power with its remaining customers.

The list forced the discussion away from statements such as "the stock used to be worth $42." It also showed why the current value might differ from the old value. A price anchor becomes dangerous when it survives without an explanation.

Next, Graham tested the proposed offer against independent alternatives. The company could buy the supplier for $30 per share, build a smaller operation internally for $14 million, or sign a three-year contract with another supplier. The internal build required more time but avoided the supplier's debt. The contract cost more per unit but preserved cash and reduced operational risk. By comparing these choices, Graham replaced a historical reference point with an opportunity-cost test: what would the company receive, and what would it give up, at each price?

The inventory review produced a similar turning point. Managers had recorded the inventory at $4.8 million because that amount represented what the company paid. Graham asked the warehouse and sales teams to estimate what customers would actually pay within ninety days. They found that $1.1 million of stock required discounts because specifications had changed. The team recorded the expected selling price after delivery and sales costs, rather than defending the original purchase cost. That decision reduced reported profit, but it gave management a more accurate view of available cash.

Graham also changed the language used in the board materials. Instead of labeling $42 the "normal price," the report called it the "prior reference price." Instead of describing the inventory reduction as a failure, it called it a "current recovery value." These labels mattered because words can preserve an anchor even after analysts update the numbers. The board could still see the past price, but the report no longer treated it as a target.

Finally, Graham introduced a delay between the first valuation and the final recommendation. Each decision-maker submitted a private estimate before the group meeting. They stated the price they believed the supplier justified and listed the two facts most likely to make that estimate wrong. The team then compared the estimates with the cash-flow model, replacement alternatives, and downside case. This process reduced the chance that the first confident opinion would set the group's range.

The board rejected the $30 offer and approved a contract with the alternative supplier. Graham's team also marked down the obsolete inventory and changed purchasing rules so future orders required a documented demand estimate. The company did not "win" by predicting the supplier's next share price. It protected cash by refusing to let an old price dictate a new decision.

What You Can Steal from Graham's Reset

Treat every old price as evidence, not truth. Write the reference price at the top of your worksheet, then place it in a separate "history" column. Build the current decision from today's sales, costs, debt, demand, and alternatives. If you value a rental property, for example, compare current rent, repairs, financing, and nearby listings before considering what you paid. The old price can provide context, but it cannot explain changed fundamentals.

Use a change list before you debate value. List at least five facts that changed since the price or cost that now influences you. Include customer losses, input costs, interest rates, regulation, product quality, and available substitutes when they apply. Then connect each change to revenue, cash flow, or risk. This step matters because people often defend a price without identifying the conditions that once supported it.

Run the Anchor Reset Routine before committing capital. The routine has four working documents: a current-facts sheet, an independent valuation, an alternatives comparison, and a downside case. Complete them in that order. For Graham, the alternatives comparison showed that a supply contract could preserve cash even if the acquisition appeared cheaper than the supplier's former market price. The routine works because it replaces one emotionally prominent number with several decision-relevant comparisons.

Separate purchase cost from recoverable value. A cost tells you what you gave up; it does not tell you what you can recover. Review inventory, equipment, investments, and business assets using expected cash proceeds after selling costs, taxes, repairs, and time. If you paid \$100 for an item that now sells for \$70, repeating "I need \$100" does not restore the missing value. It only delays recognition and may encourage you to commit more money to the same mistake.

Create a written exit or review rule before the anchor returns. Set a date and conditions that trigger reassessment. Graham could require a quarterly review of customer concentration, cash generation, debt costs, and equipment spending. An investor might review a holding when its earnings outlook changes, not merely when its price falls below the purchase price. A business owner might reduce a product line after two review periods of negative contribution margin. The rule prevents the original price from becoming the only reason to continue.

Prices help markets coordinate exchange, but remembered prices can distort judgment when conditions change. Graham's discipline did not require perfect forecasting. It required him to ask a more useful question: what do the current facts support now? That question turns a historical number from a command into information - and leaves room for money, assets, and markets to reveal their actual value.

CHAPTER 23

Confirmation Bias and Information Diets

Choose Whether You Want Evidence or Confirmation

> "The first duty of an intelligent person is to examine the evidence, not defend the conclusion."

A financial decision often begins with a sentence that sounds like a question but is really a preference: "Is this stock undervalued?" Once you ask it that way, your research tends to collect support. You notice the low price-to-earnings ratio, the confident management interview, and the favorable analyst note. You give less attention to falling cash flow, rising debt, or a competitor taking customers. The danger does not come from a lack of information. It comes from arranging information to protect an existing belief.

Confirmation bias matters because financial losses often begin before the purchase. If you decide that a currency, stock, property, or business deserves your money, you can unconsciously turn research into a defense brief. You may read five favorable articles and call yourself informed, while one inconvenient filing contains the fact that changes the decision. Market history provides repeated examples of this pattern. Investors treated Palm's public offering as proof of a new technology order while overlooking the pricing relationship between Palm and its parent company, 3Com. The attractive story drew attention; the contradictory valuation received less.

Elena, a 31-year-old analyst, faces this choice when she considers buying shares in a fast-growing payment company. The company reports rising revenue and expanding merchant adoption. Elena can research until she feels comfortable, or she can design a process that must search for evidence capable of making her abandon the purchase. The first approach feels efficient, but it rewards confidence. The second takes more discipline, yet it protects her capital from a polished story supported by selective facts.

Compare Research Methods That Test Your Belief

You can examine an investment through several workable methods. The important distinction involves what each method does with evidence that conflicts with your initial view.

Approach	How it handles disconfirming evidence	Cost	Time	Difficulty	Best for
Support-first research	Searches mainly for evidence that supports the original thesis	Low	30-60 minutes	Low	A quick first look, not a final decision
Balanced checklist	Reviews both supporting and opposing evidence using fixed questions	Low	2-4 hours	Moderate	Most personal investment decisions
The Contradiction Quota	Requires a set number of credible challenges and a written response before action	Low to moderate	4-8 hours	Moderate to high	Concentrated investments and uncertain markets

Support-first research has one legitimate use: it helps you learn the basic case quickly. If you hear about a company for the first time, you need to understand its product, customers, revenue source, and competitors. The method fails when you mistake familiarity for proof. Reading only favorable material increases confidence without increasing accuracy.

A balanced checklist improves the process by forcing a second view. You might ask what could damage revenue, whether the company depends on one customer, and what would make the current valuation unreasonable. The checklist works well for ordinary decisions, but people can still answer its questions defensively. They may write weak objections and strong supporting points.

The Contradiction Quota addresses that weakness. Before Elena buys the payment company, she must find three credible facts or arguments that challenge her thesis. "Some people dislike the stock" does not count. A qualifying contradiction must connect to value: a customer-loss risk, a cash-flow problem, a legal exposure, a pricing assumption, or a competitor with a credible advantage. She must then record whether each contradiction changes the expected return, the risk, the timing, or the position size.

The quota does not require pessimism. It requires contact with reality. A contradiction may fail to overturn the thesis. For example, Elena may discover that the company's operating margin fell because it invested in infrastructure, while cash collections remained strong and management provided a measurable path to improvement. That evidence still matters. It gives her a reasoned response instead of a vague feeling that "the market is overreacting."

Use The Contradiction Quota Before You Commit Capital

For most readers, the best choice is The Contradiction Quota. If you are just starting out, use three contradictions before any purchase because the rule remains simple enough to follow and strong enough to expose obvious errors. If you plan to invest a large share of your savings, raise the quota to five and require at least one primary source, such as a company filing, government document, contract, or audited financial statement. If you lack time, do not reduce the quota to zero; reduce the position size and delay the decision.

The decision flowchart is direct. If you cannot state your investment thesis in one sentence, stop and gather basic facts. If you can state it, find three credible contradictions. If all three contradictions concern minor issues and your written responses rely on evidence, continue to valuation and position sizing. If one contradiction threatens revenue, solvency, legal standing, or the central reason for ownership, stop and reassess. If the contradiction remains unresolved, do not buy. If the evidence conflicts because the sources use different dates or definitions, reconcile the facts before reaching a conclusion.

Apply the same process to currency and barter-related decisions. If a local business accepts payment in goods or foreign currency, do not focus only on the apparent exchange value. Search for contradictions involving storage, resale, taxes, price volatility, and the time required to convert the item into money. A contractor who accepts equipment instead of cash may receive an asset worth $2,000 in a catalog but only $1,200 in a local resale market. The contradiction is not a technical detail; it changes the payment's real value.

Use source quality as part of the test. A promotional article can suggest a question, but it should rarely settle one. A company's filing can establish reported revenue, while an industry buyer, supplier, or competitor may reveal pressure that management does not emphasize. Elena should record the source, publication date, exact claim, and the number that supports it. That record prevents a common error: remembering the conclusion while forgetting the evidence.

Build and Run Your Research File

Use one document or spreadsheet for every serious decision. Keep the structure fixed so that enthusiasm cannot quietly change the questions.

1. **Write the thesis before opening research tabs.** State the claim in one sentence and attach a time frame. Elena writes: "The payment company can grow revenue and reach sustainable cash generation within three years because small merchants continue adopting its platform." Add the intended purchase price, planned holding period, and maximum loss you can accept.

2. **List the conditions that must be true.** Break the thesis into testable claims. Elena needs merchant growth, repeat transaction volume, manageable customer-acquisition costs, adequate cash, and a path from revenue to cash generation. If the thesis depends on five conditions, one failed condition may matter more than several favorable headlines.

3. **Set the Contradiction Quota before researching.** Use three contradictions for a normal purchase and five for a concentrated position. Write the categories first: demand, competition, finances, management, regulation, valuation, and timing. This step prevents you from selecting only the easiest objections.

4. **Search deliberately for opposing evidence.** Use search terms that challenge the thesis: "customer churn," "cash flow," "debt maturity," "regulatory action," "competitor pricing," and "failed guidance." Read the company's latest annual and quarterly filings, then compare management claims with reported cash flow and customer data. Search independent sources after reviewing company material, not instead of it.

5. **Record each contradiction in a separate row.** Include the claim, source, date, supporting figure, likely effect, and your response. For Elena, a contradiction might read: "Merchant growth slowed while sales spending increased." Her response must explain whether the slowdown reflects a temporary market change or a weakening product, and what future evidence would distinguish those possibilities.

6. **Assign each contradiction a decision status.** Mark it as resolved, unresolved, or thesis-breaking. "Resolved" means reliable evidence explains the issue and preserves the thesis. "Unresolved" means the available evidence cannot settle it. "Thesis-breaking" means the issue attacks a condition that the decision requires. Never convert "unresolved" into "resolved" merely because you still like the asset.

7. **Write the strongest case against ownership.** Limit yourself to one page. Explain why a careful investor might refuse the purchase, including the most damaging number or fact. Then write the strongest response using evidence rather than optimism. If your response says "the market will recover" or "management sounds confident," the contradiction remains open.

8. **Choose the action only after the test.** Buy only when the thesis survives the quota, the valuation leaves room for error, and the position size matches the uncertainty. If the evidence remains mixed, wait for a specific condition, such as two quarters of improving cash flow or a confirmed regulatory decision. A waiting rule turns uncertainty into a manageable research task.

9. **Schedule a contradiction review.** Set a date before buying. Review the thesis after each earnings report, major filing, regulatory announcement, or sharp price move. Do not let a rising price count as confirmation; price can rise while the underlying thesis weakens.

Start today with this short checklist:

- Write one current investment thesis in a single sentence. - Set a Contradiction Quota of three credible challenges. - Find one primary source and one independent source for the decision. - Record the strongest fact that could make you wrong. - Define the exact condition that would make you wait, reduce the position, or walk away.

A sound research process does not eliminate uncertainty, and it does not guarantee a profitable decision. It does something more practical: it prevents your preferred conclusion from controlling which facts enter the decision. In barter, credit, currency, and asset markets alike, value depends on what survives exchange with reality. Your research should perform that exchange before your money does.

CHAPTER 24

Herding, Social Proof, and Momentum Traps

When the Crowd Becomes the Risk

Ruth, a 42-year-old marketing lead, watches a company's share price rise every morning while financial news, social posts, and group chats repeat the same message: the business has become "unstoppable." The company's sales have not changed enough to justify the price, but the crowd keeps buying. Ruth feels pressure to act before the opportunity disappears. That pressure is the market signal she needs to examine - not obey.

Crowding occurs when many investors respond to the same story, trade, or price pattern at the same time. Social proof makes the behavior appear safer because other people already participate. Momentum then reinforces the impression: rising prices attract buyers, buying pushes prices higher, and the higher price becomes evidence for the original decision. Fundamentals may still matter, but they can lose control of the price for long periods.

This matters to anyone building wealth through shares, funds, digital assets, property, or a small business exposed to market prices. The goal is not to avoid every popular investment. The goal is to identify when media attention and coordinated buying have overwhelmed cash flow, valuation, liquidity, or your own risk limits. The Crowd-Pressure Gauge provides a practical way to separate useful information from crowd-generated urgency.

The Crowd-Pressure Gauge Score an investment across attention, price behavior, valuation, ownership concentration, and liquidity. You can build the gauge in a spreadsheet at no cost; a basic spreadsheet application is sufficient.

Price and volume history Download at least twelve months of daily price and trading-volume data from a regulated exchange, broker, or finance platform. Free data often works for screening, but verify unusual moves against a second source before acting.

Fundamental record Collect revenue, operating profit, debt, cash, share count, and management forecasts from company filings or investor reports. Public filings usually cost nothing and provide a stronger reference than promotional articles.

Media-cycle log Record the date, headline, source, claim, and market reaction for major news items. A simple document or spreadsheet prevents memory from turning repeated headlines into false confirmation.

Position and exit worksheet Write down your entry price, maximum loss, position size, exit conditions, and review date before you buy. This costs nothing, but it removes decisions from the most emotional part of the trade.

Liquidity check Review the average daily trading value, bid-ask spread, and your ability to sell without moving the price. Your broker supplies transaction details; do not assume a popular asset remains liquid during a sell-off.

Independent valuation range Estimate a reasonable value using conservative assumptions for sales growth, margins, debt, and cash generation. A spreadsheet works better than a single target price because it shows how sensitive the result is to changing assumptions.

The tools work together. Price data shows what the crowd is doing. Fundamental records show what the business produces. The media log shows how attention changes. The position worksheet shows whether a wrong decision can damage your broader financial plan. No single measure can identify a momentum trap reliably.

Ruth could use the gauge after a week of headlines about a technology company. The price has doubled in a short period, trading volume has surged, and every article repeats the same growth forecast. Meanwhile, revenue has grown more slowly, the valuation depends on several years of unusually strong profits, and many recent buyers entered after the largest gains. The gauge would not automatically call the company worthless. It would identify a crowded trade that requires a smaller position, a higher margin of safety, or no purchase.

The Crowd-Pressure Gauge Playbook

1. **Freeze the impulse for one full trading day.** Do not buy or sell because of a single headline, viral post, or dramatic price move. The pause creates a record of the original pressure and reduces the chance that urgency will substitute for analysis.

2. **Write the crowd's claim in one sentence.** State exactly what buyers believe, such as "This company will dominate its market within three years." A precise claim gives you something testable instead of a vague feeling that the asset is "hot."

3. **Measure attention before measuring value.** Count the number of major headlines, repeated phrases, search interest if available, and references across investor communities during the past

thirty days. A sharp rise in attention alongside a sharp price rise indicates crowd participation, not proof of improving fundamentals.

4. **Compare the price move with business results.** Place the twelve-month price change beside changes in revenue, operating profit, free cash flow, debt, and share count. If the price has moved far faster than the business, mark the difference as a pressure signal requiring deeper review.

5. **Separate new information from repeated information.** Label each media item as new evidence, interpretation, or repetition. Ten articles repeating one management forecast do not equal ten independent confirmations.

6. **Check whether the story depends on one forecast.** Reduce the key assumption - such as sales growth, profit margin, or adoption speed - and recalculate value. If a small change turns an attractive valuation into an unattractive one, treat the investment as fragile.

7. **Inspect ownership and trading concentration.** Review whether a small group of funds, insiders, or recent buyers controls a large portion of available shares. Concentration can amplify both buying and selling because similar decisions may occur at the same time.

8. **Test liquidity under stress.** Assume you must sell during a day when trading volume falls and the spread widens. Estimate the price impact and the time required to exit. If you cannot exit without serious damage, reduce the position before entering.

9. **Score the Crowd-Pressure Gauge.** Give one point for each condition: rapidly rising attention, price far ahead of business results, repeated rather than new evidence, fragile valuation assumptions,

concentrated ownership, unusually high volume, and poor stressed liquidity. A score of zero to two suggests ordinary attention; three to four calls for caution; five or more signals a crowded momentum trade.

10. **Set a position size from the score, not from excitement.** For a score of three or four, cap the position at an amount that cannot disrupt your financial plan. For a score of five or more, wait for stronger evidence or avoid the trade. The exact amount depends on your finances, but the rule must exist before the price moves against you.

11. **Define the invalidation point.** Write the specific evidence that would disprove your purchase thesis: slower sales, falling margins, canceled contracts, rising debt, or a broken product promise. A falling price alone may not disprove the business case, while deteriorating cash flow may.

12. **Choose a review date before buying.** Review the thesis after the next earnings report, regulatory decision, product launch, or other defined event. A scheduled review prevents continuous exposure to a fading story simply because the crowd remains loud.

13. **Track price action without treating it as proof.** Record whether the asset rises on heavy volume, falls on heavy volume, or moves without broad participation. Momentum can continue after fundamentals weaken, so use price behavior as a warning signal rather than a business forecast.

14. **Sell or reduce when your written conditions occur.** Act on the evidence you defined before the trade. Do not replace a failed thesis with a new explanation created after the price falls.

15. **Review the decision, not only the result.** Compare your original assumptions with later facts. A profitable trade can still reflect poor process if the crowd carried it, and a losing trade can reflect sound analysis if you controlled the risk and tested the evidence.

Crowd pressure often appears most clearly when the market gives investors contradictory signals. A company may announce strong sales while its valuation assumes even stronger results for years. A popular asset may attract enormous attention while its liquidity depends on continuous new buyers. A fund may follow momentum rules that worked in calm conditions, then face forced selling when prices reverse and lenders demand more cash.

The 3Com and Palm episode illustrates the danger of a popular story overpowering basic pricing logic. Palm traded at a value that implied a negative value for the rest of 3Com, even though 3Com owned the Palm shares. Arbitrageurs recognized the mismatch, but short-selling limits, timing uncertainty, and intense demand for Palm prevented an immediate correction. The market could identify the mistake and still fail to correct it quickly. That distinction matters: recognizing mispricing does not guarantee safe timing.

The same problem appeared during the August 2007 quant crisis. Many funds held similar statistical and momentum positions. When several began selling, their trades pushed down the same securities held by other funds, which then sold to meet financing demands. The original strategy did not need to become fundamentally wrong for the crowd to create losses. Shared positioning and forced selling supplied the mechanism.

Ruth's practical response would involve no prediction about the next headline. She would record the claim, compare the price with operating results, test a weaker forecast, inspect liquidity, and score the gauge. If the score reached five, she would either avoid the purchase or use a position small enough to preserve her wider investment plan. That decision respects uncertainty instead of pretending that confidence can remove it.

Quick Reference for Crowded Markets

Attention surge: If headlines, repeated phrases, and investor discussion rise sharply, treat attention as a risk signal - not confirmation.

Price versus business: If the price rises much faster than revenue, profit, or cash flow, test the valuation under weaker assumptions.

Repeated evidence: If ten sources repeat one forecast, count it as one forecast.

Momentum: If price rises mainly because more buyers expect price rises, label the trade momentum-driven and reduce reliance on the story.

Crowd-Pressure Gauge score: Zero to two means ordinary monitoring; three to four means smaller size and stronger evidence; five or more means wait, reduce, or avoid.

Liquidity: If you cannot sell during a stressed session without a large price concession, the position is too large.

Concentration: If many owners appear to follow the same strategy, expect correlated selling when conditions change.

Valuation fragility: If a modest reduction in growth or margin destroys the investment case, demand a larger margin of safety.

Written thesis: If you cannot state what would prove you wrong, do not buy.

Media response: If a headline changes your decision immediately, pause for one trading day and update the evidence log first.

Exit rule: If the business evidence invalidates the thesis, reduce or close the position; do not wait for the crowd to agree.

Process review: If a trade succeeds only because attention kept rising, classify the result as luck or momentum exposure rather than proof of analytical skill.

Crowds can move prices beyond what fundamentals justify, and they can keep them there longer than a disciplined investor expects. The practical defense does not require perfect timing. It requires a written claim, independent evidence, a measured Crowd-Pressure Gauge, and a position size that leaves room for the crowd to be wrong. Money becomes safer when you treat popularity as a force to measure rather than a reason to follow.

CHAPTER 25

Availability and Recency: The News Loop

Why the News Loop Distorts Financial Judgment

Calista, a 28-year-old podcast host, watched a technology stock fall sharply after a widely reported data breach. Within an hour, her news feed showed the same event from several angles: the company's lost customers, angry regulators, worried employees, and analysts cutting price targets. The coverage made the breach feel like a new kind of permanent threat. Calista considered selling every technology holding she owned.

The event was real. The conclusion was not yet established. News repetition increased the event's mental availability - the ease with which she could recall it - and its recency made it feel more predictive than older, quieter evidence. A vivid loss can therefore replace a probability estimate without the investor noticing the substitution.

The practical problem is not that news matters. News can change a company's earnings, a currency's demand, or an asset's expected cash flow. The problem arises when the latest event becomes the entire forecast. The Base-Rate Backstop gives you a disciplined way to separate what happened recently from what usually happens across comparable cases. After applying it, you can classify an event, estimate a reasonable range of outcomes, and decide whether the price already reflects the news.

How the Base-Rate Backstop Works

A base rate describes how often a similar event produced a particular outcome in comparable situations. It does not predict the next result with certainty. It establishes a starting point before you adjust for evidence that makes the current case different.

Use the Base-Rate Backstop in four steps:

1. **Name the event precisely.** Replace "the market is in trouble" with a specific statement such as "the company disclosed a security breach that may increase legal costs and customer cancellations." Precision prevents emotional headlines from controlling the analysis.

2. **Find comparable cases.** Search company filings, exchange records, industry reports, and long-term price histories for similar events. Compare breaches with breaches, currency controls with currency controls, and liquidity shocks with liquidity shocks. A broad category produces a weak base rate.

3. **Measure the usual range of outcomes.** Record what happened after comparable events over a defined period, such as one month, six months, and two years. Track operating results, not only prices. A share price may fall immediately and recover later, while the underlying business continues to weaken - or the reverse.

4. **Adjust for differences, then set a decision rule.** Ask which facts make the current case better or worse than the comparable cases. Write the adjustment before you trade. For example, a breach involving encrypted data and rapid disclosure differs materially from one involving exposed payment information and delayed reporting.

The order matters. If you start with the latest headline, you will search for evidence that supports your first reaction. If you start with comparable cases, you give older and less vivid information a place in the decision.

Consider a currency crisis. A recent devaluation may lead you to expect another immediate collapse. The base rate might show that countries with large foreign-currency debt and shrinking reserves often face further pressure, while countries with manageable debt and credible fiscal action often stabilize. The recent devaluation remains important, but the comparison tells you which details deserve weight.

Do not confuse a base rate with a fixed rule. A company with a strong balance sheet may not resemble the average company in an industry. A central bank may respond faster than its historical counterparts. The backstop does not eliminate judgment; it prevents judgment from beginning with an emotionally selected example.

Applying the Backstop to a Real Decision

Calista's technology holding represented $6,000 of her $40,000 investment account. After the breach, the stock dropped from $50 to $42. She had heard three analysts predict further losses, and her podcast audience began asking whether technology companies could still protect customer data.

She applied the framework before selling.

1. **Define the event.** Calista wrote: "A listed software company disclosed unauthorized access to customer records, faces a possible regulatory fine, and has not yet reported a material increase in cancellations." This statement separated confirmed facts from forecasts.

2. **Set the comparison group.** She reviewed 12 publicly documented breaches involving software companies with subscription

revenue. She excluded retailers, banks, and cases where the company had already entered bankruptcy proceedings. The narrower group produced more useful comparisons.

3. **Record the outcomes.** She noted each company's share-price change after one month and six months, customer-retention disclosures, legal costs, and revenue growth. The results varied widely: some companies recovered after the initial decline, while others lost major customers and required several years to rebuild trust.

4. **Identify the current company's position.** The company had no reported customer cancellations, held $900 million in cash, and carried $250 million in debt. Its breach affected account information but not stored payment details. Management disclosed the incident within five days and hired an outside investigator.

5. **Make the adjustment explicit.** Those facts placed the company above the average case in financial resilience and response speed. The absence of confirmed cancellations did not prove that customers would stay, but it weakened the most severe comparison.

6. **Separate price judgment from business judgment.** Calista estimated that a $3 per share decline could reflect higher legal costs and slower sales. She could not justify the market's implied assumption that the company's entire subscription model had failed. She chose to reduce the position from $6,000 to $4,500 rather than sell everything, then scheduled a review after the next earnings report.

7. **Write the update conditions.** She would reconsider if customer cancellations exceeded management's previous retention range, if regulators imposed a major penalty, or if new disclosures showed payment information had been exposed. She would not

change the position merely because another headline repeated the original breach.

The expected outcome was not a guaranteed profit. The process improved the quality of the decision by matching the size of the response to the evidence. It also protected Calista from a common error: selling after a vivid event, then buying back later at a higher price when the news cycle quieted.

Quick checklist

- State exactly what happened and separate facts from predictions. - Compare the event with cases from the same industry and asset type. - Record outcomes over more than one time period. - Check whether the current balance sheet and management response differ from the comparison group. - Write the facts that would change your view. - Set a review date instead of reacting to every new headline. - Limit financial exposure while uncertainty remains high.

A useful worksheet can fit on one page:

Question	Calista's entry
Confirmed event	Unauthorized access to customer records
Comparable cases	12 software-company breaches
Current financial position	$900 million cash; $250 million debt
Immediate price move	$50 to $42
Evidence of lasting damage	No confirmed cancellations yet
Review triggers	Retention decline, major penalty, broader exposure

This record creates friction between the headline and the trade. That friction has value because it gives the base rate time to challenge the most available example.

What to Watch For in the News Loop

The headline becomes the forecast

A dramatic headline often compresses several claims into one emotional impression. "Company faces crisis" may mean a temporary investigation, a serious operating problem, or an existential threat. Those outcomes require different probabilities and different actions.

Do this: Rewrite the headline as a testable claim, then identify the evidence that would confirm or reject it.

Not this: Treat repeated coverage as independent evidence. Ten articles quoting the same filing still represent one underlying fact.

The comparison group hides important differences

A base rate becomes misleading when the cases do not share the features that drive the outcome. A breach involving payment credentials cannot automatically establish the likely effect of a breach involving encrypted contact information. Likewise, a currency collapse under a fixed exchange rate may not predict a move under a floating system.

Do this: Record the selection rules for your comparison group before reviewing the outcomes. Include the cases you might prefer to exclude.

Not this: Choose only famous examples that support your first impression.

The investor updates too quickly

A fresh development can matter, but constant updates create a second form of recency bias. Each new rumor feels like a reason to revise the forecast, even when it adds no new information. Calista's rule - review at the next earnings report unless a defined trigger appears - protected her from turning every alert into a transaction.

Do this: Separate information that changes the probability from information that merely repeats the event. Use filings, earnings releases, and official statements for major decisions.

Not this: Change a position because the news cycle has become louder.

The Base-Rate Backstop does not ask you to ignore recent events. It asks you to place them in proportion. A breach, devaluation, failed product launch, or sudden market loss may change the outlook, but the size of that change depends on comparable evidence, current conditions, and the price already in the market. When you make those three elements visible, vivid news loses its power to masquerade as certainty. That discipline turns the news loop from a trading command into an input for better judgment.

CHAPTER 26

Mental Accounting and Risk Buckets

The Hidden Portfolio Behind Separate Income Streams

What would change if every dollar tied to your work, investments, and future income appeared on one balance sheet? Owen, a 37-year-old engineer, earned a $118,000 salary, received a performance bonus that varied between $8,000 and $18,000, and held $42,000 in investments. He treated these sources as separate worlds. His salary funded ordinary life, his bonus paid for large purchases, and his investment account carried the risk he considered "acceptable."

That arrangement looked orderly, but it created an uneven portfolio. Owen's salary depended on one employer and one specialized career. His bonus depended on the same employer. His investments added market risk on top of that employment risk. When his bonus arrived, he spent it quickly because he viewed it as extra money. When his investments gained value, he took larger positions because those gains felt less earned than his salary.

The key insight is simple: salary, bonuses, and investment gains are different cash flows, but they belong to one risk system. Treating them as separate accounts can cause you to take too much risk precisely when your total financial exposure has already increased.

Money has always required a unit of account. Barter fails when people cannot agree on equivalent values; modern households create a similar problem when they measure each income source by a different mental standard. A salary becomes "safe," a bonus becomes "free," and a gain becomes "house money." The labels change the decisions even though every dollar can pay the same bill.

The One-Pot Portfolio Rule corrects this error. Place all assets, liabilities, income claims, and planned spending into one financial picture. Then assign risk according to the whole picture rather than according to the account where money happens to sit.

Principles for One-Pot Risk Control

1. Count employment income as an asset with concentration risk.

A job produces future cash flow, so it has economic value. You cannot sell your salary like a bond, but losing it can affect your finances more severely than a temporary market decline. If your salary, bonus, pension, stock grants, and career prospects all depend on one employer or industry, your household already holds a concentrated position.

Owen worked in industrial automation. His salary depended on manufacturing demand, his bonus depended on company results, and his professional network sat largely inside the same sector. Buying more industrial companies because he understood them would not diversify him. It would increase the same exposure already embedded in his income.

Count that exposure before choosing investments. You do not need a precise valuation of your career. You need an honest classification: stable, cyclical, concentrated, or uncertain. A tenured public-sector role may support more investment risk than a commission-heavy job in a volatile industry. The reason is not prestige or income level; it is the reliability and concentration of future cash flow.

2. Treat every dollar as earned capital once it enters the household.

A bonus, tax refund, inheritance, and investment gain may feel different from wages, but they have identical purchasing power after they arrive. Calling a bonus "extra" encourages immediate spending. Calling a gain "house money" encourages speculative trades. Both reactions ignore the opportunity cost: money used today cannot strengthen reserves, reduce debt, or fund a diversified portfolio.

Assign each inflow a job before it arrives. Use a written rule such as: 50 percent of a bonus goes to long-term investments, 30 percent goes to cash reserves or debt reduction, and 20 percent supports planned spending. The exact split depends on your debt, reserves, and employment risk. The important feature is that the rule applies before emotion enters the decision.

This approach also prevents gains from becoming a separate casino. If an investment rises from $20,000 to $30,000, the additional $10,000 belongs to the same household portfolio as the original capital. Decide whether to keep, rebalance, or spend it by examining total exposure - not by asking whether the gain feels real.

3. Set risk limits for the whole pot, not each account.

A retirement account can appear diversified while the household remains highly exposed to one outcome. Owen held broad market funds, company stock, and cash, but his job already tied him to the industrial economy. Looking only at the investment account hid the concentration.

Set limits across all meaningful exposures. These may include one employer, one industry, one country, one property market, or one highly volatile asset. Then review the limits after salary changes, bonuses, major gains, job moves, and debt increases. Risk changes when the household balance sheet changes.

A whole-pot limit also creates consistency. You stop saying, "I can afford to gamble with the bonus," when the bonus represents a large share of your annual savings. You stop increasing stock exposure after a market gain merely because the original contribution feels protected.

4. Match risk to the purpose and timing of the money.

Money needed within two or three years should not depend on a favorable market exit. Money intended for retirement several decades away can tolerate more price movement, provided your income and reserves can withstand a downturn. The same investment can therefore be suitable for one purpose and unsuitable for another.

Separate risk by time and purpose, then reconnect the buckets through the One-Pot Portfolio Rule. A short-term reserve protects the whole portfolio from forced selling. A long-term investment bucket supports growth. A discretionary spending bucket allows enjoyment without disguising consumption as investment. These buckets organize decisions, but the total risk still requires one review.

Applying the One-Pot Portfolio Rule

Owen wanted to invest a $12,000 annual bonus. Before applying the rule, he planned to place the entire amount into a technology fund because his salary covered his bills and his existing investments had recently performed well. That decision treated the bonus as independent capital.

He followed these steps instead:

1. **List every major financial input and obligation.** Owen recorded his $118,000 salary, expected $12,000 bonus, $42,000 investment account, $16,000 cash reserve, $210,000 mortgage, and monthly household spending of $5,200. He also noted that both salary and bonus depended on his engineering employer.

2. **Classify the employment exposure.** His salary covered roughly 23 months of household spending before taxes, but the income could fall if the company reduced staff or canceled bonuses. Owen marked his employment exposure as concentrated rather than fully secure. That classification mattered because his proposed technology fund would add risk without reducing dependence on his employer.

3. **Set the reserve target before investing.** Owen chose a nine-month reserve because his industry could experience long hiring gaps and his bonus was uncertain. Nine months of $5,200 required $46,800. With $16,000 already saved, he needed $30,800 more before treating the full bonus as long-term investment capital.

4. **Assign the bonus before receiving it.** Owen directed $6,000 to the reserve, $3,600 to mortgage principal, and $2,400 to a diversified investment fund. The allocation reflected his actual position: uncertain employment income, a large fixed debt, and an existing investment account.

5. **Review total exposure rather than the new account alone.** His investment account contained $24,000 in a broad stock fund, $10,000 in company shares, and $8,000 in a technology fund. The new $2,400 went to the broad fund, not the technology fund. He also set a rule that company shares could not exceed 10 percent of his investable

assets. If future stock grants pushed the holding above that limit, he would sell the excess according to his tax and account rules.

6. **Create a gains rule.** If the portfolio rose by $8,000 or more above its planned allocation, Owen would rebalance rather than automatically increase risk. If he needed money for a purchase within two years, he would move that amount into cash rather than rely on continued market gains.

The difference between the two approaches was substantial:

Decision point	Separate-world approach	One-Pot Portfolio Rule
Bonus invested in technology fund	$12,000	$0
Bonus added to cash reserve	$0	$6,000
Bonus used for mortgage reduction	$0	$3,600
Bonus invested broadly	$0	$2,400
Employer-related exposure	Ignored	Included in risk review
Response to future gains	Take more risk	Rebalance to limits

After the change, Owen did not eliminate risk. He made it visible and intentional. His reserve became stronger, his debt declined, and his investment contribution continued. Most importantly, a future bonus no longer created a fresh argument about what the money "felt like." The rule decided before the cash arrived.

Review the one-pot picture at least twice a year and after any major change. Update salary dependence, bonus expectations, investment values, debt, cash reserves, and planned spending. A simple spreadsheet works. Use columns for asset or income source, current value, purpose, time horizon, and main risk. Add a note for concentrated exposures such as employer stock or industry-specific income.

Troubleshooting Uneven Risk Decisions

Problem: Owen invests his salary cautiously but takes speculative risks with bonuses and gains.

Why it happens: He assigns moral value to the source of the money. Salary feels earned and therefore protected; a bonus feels unexpected; a gain feels less painful to lose. This mental accounting changes his risk tolerance without changing his financial capacity.

Fix: Write the allocation rule before the bonus or gain arrives. Direct each inflow into the same categories - reserves, debt reduction, long-term investment, and planned spending. For gains, compare the current holding with the whole-pot limit. If a position exceeds its limit, rebalance it even when the gain feels like a reward. Keep a small, explicitly labeled speculation allowance if you want one, and cap it in dollars rather than letting it expand with excitement.

Problem: His investment account appears diversified, but his household depends on one employer and one industry.

Why it happens: Account statements show financial assets, not the value and risk of future earnings. A broad fund cannot fully offset the danger of losing concentrated employment income, especially when the same economic cycle affects both the job and the investments.

Fix: Add employment income to the risk review. Mark the job as stable, cyclical, concentrated, or uncertain. Avoid adding large positions that rise and fall for the same reasons as your income. Build a larger cash reserve when replacing the job would take time. Direct employer stock grants into a separate concentration limit, then reduce the holding when it exceeds that limit.

Problem: Owen keeps changing the rules when markets move or a bonus arrives.

Why it happens: A flexible rule can become no rule at all. Market gains create overconfidence, while losses create fear. Treating each event as unique lets current emotion override the household's actual time horizon and obligations.

Fix: Schedule a one-pot review on a fixed date, such as the first weekend of January and July. Outside those reviews, make changes only when a defined trigger occurs: job loss, a major debt change, a new financial goal within two years, or an exposure that exceeds its limit. Record the reason for every change. If the reason reads "the market feels different," wait until the scheduled review unless your cash needs have changed.

The One-Pot Portfolio Rule does not require identical treatment for every dollar. Short-term reserves should remain safer than retirement assets, and planned spending should not compete with emergency cash. The rule requires one honest accounting system underneath those decisions. Salary, bonuses, and gains may arrive through different doors, but they enter the same household economy. Once you measure them together, risk stops drifting with the source of the money and starts following the structure of the balance sheet.

CHAPTER 27

Framing Effects in Performance Reporting

Why the Frame Changes the Decision

A report can show the same $12,000 result as a gain, a shortfall, or a warning simply by changing the comparison point. "Revenue increased by $12,000" sounds positive. "Revenue reached $88,000 against a $100,000 target" signals a problem. Both statements can be accurate, yet they lead readers toward different decisions.

Performance reporting matters because people rarely inspect every underlying transaction. They rely on headings, summaries, colors, order, and comparisons. A green arrow may encourage spending; a red variance may trigger cuts. The presentation does not alter the cash, inventory, debt, or asset value, but it can alter the action taken in response.

Before reviewing a report, gather the source figures, the comparison period, the target or budget, and the time window. A spreadsheet, accounting system, bank statement, or sales ledger can provide the figures. Do not begin with the headline. Begin by confirming what the headline measures and what it leaves outside the frame.

Nina, a 46-year-old compliance manager, reviews a monthly report showing that operating costs fell from $74,000 to $70,000. The report labels the change "cost savings." Nina checks the budget and finds a planned monthly cost of $66,000. The same $4,000 decline now represents a $4,000 overspend against plan. The wording did not create a false number; it concealed the more useful comparison.

The central task is to separate the result from its presentation. A result answers, "What happened?" A frame answers, "Compared with what, over which period, and with which interpretation?" Wealth-building decisions require both answers.

The Frame-Flip Check

The Frame-Flip Check tests whether a conclusion survives a change in wording and comparison. It does not ask you to distrust every report. It asks you to expose the choices that shape the reader's first impression.

Use the following sequence when a report presents a gain, loss, improvement, or warning.

1. **Write down the raw figures.** Record the current result, the comparison result, and the target if one exists. Keep the units clear. A revenue figure, a margin, and a cash balance cannot substitute for one another.

2. **Name the comparison.** Identify whether the report compares the result with last month, the same month last year, a budget, a forecast, or a selected benchmark. "Up" has no meaning until the comparison becomes visible.

3. **Calculate the absolute change.** Subtract the comparison figure from the current figure. If sales rose from $80,000 to $88,000, the absolute change equals $8,000.

4. **Calculate the rate of change.** Divide the absolute change by the comparison figure. In this example, $8,000 divided by $80,000 equals 0.10, or 10%. State the calculation so the reader can check it.

5. **Flip the frame.** Rewrite the headline from at least two other valid viewpoints. Compare the result with the target, the prior period, and the relevant cost or cash measure. If the report says "sales up 10%," ask whether profit, cash, or units moved in the same direction.

6. **Check the denominator.** A percentage can look impressive when the starting figure is small. A rise from $2,000 to $3,000 equals $1,000, or 50%, but it may matter less than a $5,000 decline in another line.

7. **Check the time window.** A daily result, monthly result, and trailing twelve-month result answer different questions. A strong week does not prove a strong year.

8. **Rewrite the conclusion in neutral language.** State the figures, comparison, and limitation before deciding what to do.

Consider a report that states: "Investment account value increased 8%, adding $4,000." The underlying figures show a rise from $50,000 to $54,000. The Frame-Flip Check produces several valid views:

Frame	Statement	Decision risk
Prior value	Value rose from $50,000 to $54,000	May encourage further buying
Target value	Value remains $3,000 below the $57,000 target	May reveal underperformance
Contribution-adjusted	$2,500 of the increase came from new deposits	May overstate investment performance
After fees	Net value rose $3,700 after $300 in fees	May change the attractiveness of the result
Cash need	Account rose, but a $6,000 payment is due next month	May expose a liquidity problem

The neutral conclusion reads: "The account balance increased from $50,000 to $54,000, including $2,500 in new deposits and $300 in fees. The investment gain therefore requires separate calculation, and the balance remains below the $57,000 target."

This method also applies to barter and non-cash exchange. A business may report $6,000 of services received through barter as "income generated." That label can hide the value of the service provided, tax treatment, collection risk, and the fact that no cash entered the bank account. Flip the frame: record the value received, the value given, the timing, and the cash alternative. The exchange may still make sense, but the decision should not depend on a favorable label.

Try It Yourself: Nina's Compliance Report

Use a blank sheet or spreadsheet and enter the following report figures:

- Current compliance review cost: $70,000 - Prior-month cost: $74,000 - Approved monthly budget: $66,000 - Completed reviews: 140 - Prior-month completed reviews: 160 - Open high-priority findings: 18 - Prior-month open high-priority findings: 12 - Cash paid during the month: $62,000

The report headline says, "Compliance costs reduced by $4,000 while activity remained strong." Apply the Frame-Flip Check.

First, calculate the cost change: $70,000 minus $74,000 equals negative $4,000. Costs fell by $4,000 against the prior month. Next, compare costs with the budget: $70,000 minus $66,000 equals a $4,000 overspend. The favorable frame uses the prior month; the unfavorable frame uses the approved plan.

Now calculate output. Completed reviews fell from 160 to 140, a decline of 20 reviews. The cost per completed review rose from

$462.50 ($74,000 divided by 160) to $500 ($70,000 divided by 140). Total cost fell, but cost per review increased.

Finally, inspect risk. Open high-priority findings rose from 12 to 18, an increase of 6 findings. Cash paid equals $62,000, which differs from the $70,000 reported cost. That difference may reflect unpaid invoices, timing, or accounting treatment. It requires explanation before anyone treats the lower cash payment as a saving.

Rewrite the report in neutral form:

"Monthly compliance cost fell from $74,000 to $70,000 but exceeded the $66,000 budget by $4,000. Completed reviews declined from 160 to 140, raising cost per review from $462.50 to $500. Open high-priority findings increased from 12 to 18. Reported cost exceeded cash paid by $8,000, so the timing difference requires reconciliation."

The expected outcome is not a prettier report. It is a decision-ready report that prevents one favorable comparison from hiding three adverse ones. Nina can now ask precise questions: Why did completed reviews fall? Why did high-priority findings rise? What explains the $8,000 difference between cost and cash paid?

Completion check:

- You recorded every raw figure. - You identified the comparison behind the headline. - You tested the result against budget, output, risk, and cash. - You rewrote the conclusion without loaded wording.

Common Framing Mistakes

Mistake: Treating a favorable comparison as the full result

A report may compare revenue with a weak prior month while ignoring the budget or the same period in the prior year. This creates a technically correct but incomplete success signal.

Do this: Show the current result beside the prior period, target, and relevant cash or profit measure. In Nina's report, display $70,000 current cost, $74,000 prior cost, and $66,000 budget in the same table.

Not this: "Costs improved," without naming the comparison.

Mistake: Confusing percentage movement with financial importance

A 50% increase from $2,000 to $3,000 may attract more attention than a $10,000 change on a larger line. Percentages describe relative movement; they do not determine economic importance by themselves.

Do this: Show both the absolute change and the percentage change. Add the starting value so the reader can judge scale.

Not this: "Performance rose 50%," without showing the underlying dollars or units.

Mistake: Mixing accounting results with cash results

Accrued costs, unpaid invoices, deposits, and asset movements can make reported performance differ from cash movement. A business can report lower costs while paying more cash, or report profit while lacking cash for a bill.

Do this: Place profit or performance figures beside cash received and cash paid, then explain timing differences. Reconcile any gap before recommending action.

Not this: "Cash improved because expenses fell," when the report only shows an accounting expense decline.

A strong performance report does more than present numbers neatly. It reveals the comparison, scale, timing, and omitted context that shape judgment. The Frame-Flip Check turns presentation from a source of hidden bias into an object of analysis. Once you can see how wording changes a decision, you can evaluate money, barter, investments, and market claims with the same discipline: identify the frame, recover the underlying exchange, and decide from the numbers rather than the headline.

CHAPTER 28

Market Anomalies: The January Effect

> "A calendar date does not create value by itself; investor behavior around that date can create a temporary price pattern."

What the January Effect Reveals

The **January effect** describes a recurring tendency for certain stocks - especially smaller companies that declined near year-end - to rebound during January. The pattern attracted attention because the move often appeared stronger than ordinary day-to-day market noise. It also raised a practical question: if investors could observe the pattern, why did competition not remove it?

The answer begins with year-end behavior rather than January itself. **Tax-loss selling** occurs when investors sell an investment that has fallen below its purchase price to realize a capital loss. That loss can offset taxable capital gains, subject to the investor's tax rules. Investors often complete those sales before the calendar year closes. When January arrives, some investors buy back the stocks they sold, while other buyers step in because the forced selling has ended.

Small-cap stocks are shares of companies with relatively modest market values. They often trade less actively than large companies, so a determined wave of selling can push their prices down more sharply. **Large-cap stocks**, by contrast, represent much bigger companies with deeper trading markets. Their prices usually absorb year-end selling more easily because more buyers and sellers participate.

The January effect therefore reflects a combination of tax timing, portfolio reporting, liquidity, and investor attention. It never guaranteed a profitable trade. A stock sold for tax reasons may also have genuine business problems. The pattern weakened among large-cap stocks because professional investors noticed it, trading became cheaper and faster, and large companies attracted enough year-round demand to reduce the impact of temporary selling.

Breaking Down the Historical Pattern

The Tax-Window Attribution framework separates the January effect into four questions: what caused the December selling, how much selling pressure reached the market, whether January demand reversed it, and whether the pattern survived after trading costs and risk.

First, identify the likely year-end tax window. An investor who bought a stock at $40 and watched it fall to $25 may sell before December ends to record a $15 loss. That decision can make sense for tax planning, but it does not prove that the stock deserves a January rebound. The company may have missed its targets, lost a major customer, or carried too much debt. Tax pressure and business deterioration can occur at the same time.

Second, examine the type of stock receiving the pressure. Small companies with limited daily trading volume can experience a sharp price decline when many investors sell at once. A $25 stock may fall to $21 not because its long-term value changed by 16 percent, but because few buyers stood ready during the tax-selling window. That price can recover when normal trading returns. Yet a thin market also creates wider spreads, larger price gaps, and greater difficulty exiting a position.

Third, separate a rebound from a durable investment case. A January rise may represent only a return toward the earlier trading range. If the stock fell from $40 to $25 and later reached $29, the investor still faced a company worth less than before the decline. A short-term recovery does not repair weak earnings or excessive debt.

Fourth, account for the **wash-sale rule**, which can restrict the immediate tax deduction when an investor sells a security at a loss and buys the same or a substantially identical security again within the restricted period. The exact treatment depends on the investor's jurisdiction and circumstances. A person who attempts to capture the January effect without checking the tax rules may create an unwanted tax result.

Large-cap stocks weakened as January-effect candidates for several specific reasons. Large companies receive continuous attention from pension funds, mutual funds, exchange-traded funds, analysts, and institutional traders. That broad participation supplies buyers when one group sells. Their shares also trade more frequently, so a temporary imbalance between sellers and buyers usually produces a smaller price distortion.

Technology reduced the remaining delay. Investors can screen thousands of securities, compare prices, and place orders quickly. Once a predictable year-end pattern becomes widely known, traders attempt to buy before the expected rebound. Their early buying moves prices sooner, reducing the return available in January. Trading costs, taxes, and the risk of holding a weak company then consume much of the apparent advantage.

The pattern also changed because professional managers care about how their portfolios look at year-end. **Window dressing** describes adjustments made near a reporting date to make holdings appear more attractive or more consistent with a stated strategy. A manager may reduce an unpopular holding before year-end, adding pressure to stocks that already fell. That pressure can reverse in January, but it can also reflect temporary presentation choices rather than a reliable market rule.

The Tax-Window Attribution framework asks you to test each explanation rather than label every January rise as an anomaly:

1. Compare the stock's December decline with its industry and the broader market. 2. Check whether the company released bad news that explains the fall. 3. Review trading volume and bid-ask spreads before entering. 4. Calculate taxes, commissions, and the cost of holding the position. 5. Define the exit before buying, because a rebound can fail quickly.

These checks protect you from confusing a calendar pattern with an investment thesis.

Making the Tax-Window Attribution Work

Harold, a 60-year-old retiree, wants to add growth to a portfolio that already contains broad-market funds and high-quality bonds. In December, he notices several small companies that fell sharply after a general market decline. He considers buying them solely because January is approaching.

Harold should not begin with a purchase. He should build a short review sheet for each candidate. Suppose one company fell from $32 to $24 during December. Harold records the reason for the decline, the company's cash position, its debt payments, recent earnings, and average daily trading volume. He also checks whether the stock fell more than comparable companies. If the entire industry suffered from a permanent demand problem, a January rebound becomes less convincing.

Next, Harold measures the trade rather than relying on a headline. He plans to invest $2,000. If the stock trades infrequently, his order could move the price. He uses a limit order - a purchase instruction that sets the highest price he will pay - rather than an unrestricted market order. He also confirms that the position will remain small enough that a failed rebound will not threaten his retirement income.

Harold then checks the tax consequences with his tax professional. He already owns the same company in a taxable account and sold part of the position at a loss earlier in the month. Buying it back too soon could affect the loss treatment. He also confirms whether his retirement account changes the analysis. This step matters because a trade that appears profitable before tax may produce little benefit after tax.

Finally, Harold writes down two outcomes. If the stock rises from $24 to $27 after the tax-selling window closes, he will review whether the original reason for buying still exists rather than automatically holding for a larger gain. If the company issues bad news or the price breaks below his predetermined risk limit, he will exit. He records the entry price, exit price, holding period, total costs, and performance against a broad-market fund.

Harold's process does not attempt to predict January perfectly. It tests whether tax-window pressure plausibly explains the decline and whether the expected rebound compensates him for company risk, liquidity risk, and taxes.

| Candidate | December decline | Likely temporary pressure | Business risk | Practical decision | |---|---:|---|---|---| | Small company with no new bad news | Sharp | Plausible | Must investigate | Consider only after review | | Large profitable company with deep trading volume | Mild | Less important | Often easier to assess | Do not rely on January alone | | Company with falling sales and rising debt | Sharp | Unclear | High | Avoid calendar-only trade | | Stock with wide bid-ask spread | Any | Trading friction may dominate | Depends on company | Use caution or skip |

Harold evaluates the result after the holding period, not merely after a favorable January session. If he earns a modest gain but pays substantial costs and accepts excessive risk, the strategy failed even if the stock rose. If he avoids a loss because his review uncovered deteriorating finances, the process succeeded by preventing a weak trade.

Lessons from a Weakened Anomaly

Takeaway: The January effect began as a behavior pattern, not a law of markets. Tax-loss selling, year-end portfolio changes, and thin trading can create temporary pressure. Those forces explain why smaller declining stocks received more attention than stable large companies. They do not guarantee that every stock will recover.

Takeaway: Large-cap markets weakened the pattern through depth and competition. Large companies attract more buyers, trade more actively, and receive constant analysis. That activity makes it harder for tax-related selling to push prices far from widely watched valuations. Once traders anticipate the pattern, their early orders reduce the later opportunity.

Takeaway: The Tax-Window Attribution framework must include taxes and business quality. A January trade can fail because the wash-sale rule changes the tax result, because trading costs consume the gain, or because the company deserved its December decline. Attribution forces you to identify the actual source of the price move before risking capital.

Key actions: screen for year-end declines, investigate company news, compare small-cap and large-cap liquidity, check tax rules, use limit orders where appropriate, keep the position modest, and define an exit before purchase. Track the result after all costs against a simple benchmark. The calendar may reveal investor behavior, but disciplined analysis decides whether that behavior offers a usable opportunity.

CHAPTER 29

Calendar Patterns and Their Modern Limits

The Calendar Effects Worth Testing

A stock index closes weak on a Monday, rises near the turn of the month, firms before a holiday, and then attracts attention every Halloween. These patterns look simple because the calendar is simple. The trading decision is not. A recurring price tendency can disappear after fees, shift into a different day, or reflect a risk that the calendar itself does not explain.

The useful question is therefore not, "Does Monday work?" It is, "After costs, taxes, spreads, and changing market conditions, does a calendar rule improve a complete trading plan?" The Calendar-to-Cost Filter answers that question. It compares the pattern's raw return with the return a real investor could keep after execution costs and risk.

Four effects deserve separate treatment. The Monday effect concerns the first trading day of the week. The turn-of-month effect concerns the final trading days of one month and the opening days of the next. Holiday effects concern trading sessions immediately before or after a market holiday. The Halloween effect refers to the old observation that markets often perform better from late autumn through spring than during the warmer months. Each effect has a different timing window, possible cause, and failure mode.

How the Calendar-to-Cost Filter Works

Start with a precise rule. "Buy around the turn of the month" does not qualify. A usable rule states the asset, entry time, exit time, position size, and treatment of holidays. For example: buy a broad-market exchange-traded fund at the close of the final trading day of a month, hold through the fourth trading day of the next month, and exit at that close. An exchange-traded fund is a pooled investment that trades throughout the day like a stock.

Then test the rule against a comparison. The comparison might hold the same fund continuously, hold it only outside the calendar window, or hold cash during the excluded sessions. Without a comparison, a calendar pattern can receive credit for a general market rise. A buy-and-hold investor may earn more than a seasonal trader even when the seasonal window shows a positive result.

Use these stages:

1. **Define the window.** Record the exact entry and exit dates for every month, Monday, holiday, or Halloween period. Treat a weekend or market closure as part of the rule, not as an inconvenience to handle later.

2. **Measure the raw result.** Calculate the price change during each window. Keep gains and losses separate. A pattern that depends on one unusually strong period deserves more suspicion than one with steadier results.

3. **Subtract realistic costs.** Include the bid-ask spread, the difference between the price available to buyers and sellers; commissions if your broker charges them; fund expenses; taxes; and the cost of cash sitting outside the market. If you trade a small account, round-trip costs can consume a meaningful part of a short holding-period gain.

4. **Check exposure.** Compare the pattern's worst decline, largest losing streak, and time in the market with the benchmark. A strategy that earns slightly more but creates a much deeper loss may not suit your account.

5. **Test stability.** Divide the record into earlier and later periods. Also test large-cap stocks, small-cap stocks, bonds, and international markets separately. If the effect appears only in one narrow sample, treat it as a research lead rather than an investment rule.

The four effects differ in practical strength. The Monday effect often appears weakest as a stand-alone trade because many traders know it and because weekend news can create large gaps in either direction. The turn-of-month effect has a clearer possible mechanism: scheduled payroll contributions, pension flows, fund rebalancing, and month-end reporting can concentrate buying or selling. Yet those flows vary across markets and can move before the calendar date.

Holiday effects can persist when trading volume falls and investor behavior changes before a closure. Thin trading can also make prices look stronger because fewer orders stand in the way of a move. The Halloween effect offers a broad seasonal allocation idea rather than a precise entry signal. Its long holding window reduces trading costs, but it also leaves the investor exposed to many ordinary market risks unrelated to the season.

Calendar dates do not create value by themselves. They may mark recurring cash flows, reporting deadlines, tax decisions, or changes in investor attention. When those causes change, the pattern can weaken or vanish. Treat the date as a clue about market behavior, not as a guarantee.

Priyam Applies the Filter

Priyam, a 39-year-old quant hobbyist, wants to compare the four effects using one broad-market exchange-traded fund. He has a $25,000 account, pays no commission, and estimates that each round trip costs 0.12 percent through spreads and execution slippage. Slippage means the difference between the price used in a test and the price the trader actually receives.

He begins with five years of daily closing prices and writes four explicit rules:

- Monday rule: buy at Friday's close and sell at Monday's close.
- Turn-of-month rule: buy at the close of the final trading day of a month and sell at the close of the fourth trading day of the next month.
- Holiday rule: buy at the close two trading sessions before a United States market holiday and sell at the close immediately before that holiday.
- Halloween rule: buy at the close of the final trading day of October and sell at the close of the final trading day of April.

Priyam avoids overlapping trades. If a holiday window overlaps the turn-of-month window, he records the overlap and tests it separately rather than counting the same return twice. He also records the benchmark return from continuous ownership.

His worksheet contains these columns:

Field	What Priyam records
Entry and exit	Exact trading dates and closing prices
Gross return	Price change before costs
Trading cost	0.12 percent for each completed round trip
Net return	Gross return minus trading cost and fund expenses
Benchmark return	Return from holding throughout the same period
Worst loss	Largest peak-to-trough decline
Losing streak	Longest sequence of losing trades
Market exposure	Portion of the test period invested

Suppose the Monday rule produces a small gross gain but loses money after the 0.12 percent round-trip cost. Priyam rejects it for his account. The result does not prove that Mondays never differ from other days. It shows that the difference does not compensate him for trading it.

Suppose the turn-of-month rule produces a larger net gain, but most of that gain comes from a single month during a sharp market rebound. Priyam marks the result as unstable. He then tests a simpler version: remain invested continuously but add no special trade. If the calendar rule fails to beat that comparison after costs, it offers no clear advantage.

The holiday rule may show a positive average while producing only a few observations each year. Priyam checks every trade, including holidays that follow major news. He also tests buying one session earlier and exiting one session earlier. A small shift can reveal whether the effect comes from the holiday itself or from positioning that occurs before it.

The Halloween rule requires a different judgment. Its six-month holding period may reduce trading friction, but it does not remove market risk. Priyam compares the seasonal rule with holding the fund continuously and with holding it from May through October. If the seasonal rule improves results mainly because it avoids a few severe declines, he records that benefit alongside the missed gains during strong summer rallies. He does not describe the rule as "safe."

After four weeks of testing, Priyam ranks the effects by net improvement over the benchmark, stability across subperiods, drawdown, and simplicity. He chooses no rule that fails the cost test or relies on one exceptional observation. If he adopts the turn-of-month rule, he starts with only part of his account, records each expected and actual fill, and reviews the results after twelve completed trades. That review period matters because a short run can produce a misleading result through chance.

The expected outcome is not a guaranteed profit. The expected outcome is a better decision: Priyam knows which pattern survives costs, how much risk it adds, and whether it deserves a small live test.

Mistakes That Destroy Calendar Tests

Treating a pattern as a prediction

The error comes from turning an average historical tendency into a promise about the next date. A weak Monday can follow a strong Monday, and a holiday rally can fail after unexpected news. Calendar effects describe conditional behavior, not certainty.

Do this: Use the pattern as one input. Confirm the asset, trend, liquidity, position size, and maximum acceptable loss. Record the trade before the date arrives so hindsight cannot change the rule.

Not this: Buy automatically because a calendar label sounds historically favorable.

Counting gross returns as spendable returns

The root cause involves ignoring short holding periods. A trade that earns 0.20 percent before costs may lose money after the spread, slippage, taxes, and fund expenses. Frequent Monday or holiday trades face this problem more often than a twice-yearly Halloween trade.

Do this: Apply the Calendar-to-Cost Filter to every completed trade. Use your actual broker costs, a conservative spread estimate, and the tax treatment that fits your account. Reject the rule when the net result fails to beat its comparison.

Not this: Copy a published calendar table without checking how its prices, execution times, and costs were calculated.

Mining the calendar until something looks impressive

The error occurs when a trader tests many windows, assets, and entry dates but reports only the best result. With enough choices, random success becomes easy to find. A Monday rule can become a Tuesday rule, then a two-day rule, until the data appears to cooperate.

Do this: Write the rule before reviewing the final results. Keep a record of every tested variation, separate earlier data from later data, and retest the chosen rule on new observations. Prefer a simple rule that remains useful after costs over a complicated rule with a higher historical return.

Not this: Change the dates after every losing trade or select the strongest calendar window from a large menu.

Quick reference: Define exact dates, compare with continuous ownership, subtract every realistic cost, measure drawdown and exposure, test more than one time period, and treat the result as a probability rather than a promise. Monday and holiday effects often require especially strict cost checks. Turn-of-month effects deserve flow and overlap analysis. Halloween effects need a benchmark and a clear discussion of missed gains and market risk. The calendar can reveal recurring behavior, but only disciplined measurement can show whether that behavior remains investable.

CHAPTER 30

Limits to Arbitrage: Why Mispricings Persist

The Mispricing That Could Not Be Bought Away

Marisol, a 34-year-old portfolio analyst, noticed what appeared to be an obvious pricing error in the public shares of 3Com and Palm. 3Com owned most of Palm, yet Palm's market value implied that 3Com's remaining businesses had a negative value. The law of one price suggested a straightforward trade: buy 3Com, short Palm, and wait for the relationship to correct.

The arithmetic looked cleaner than the trade. Palm had become a fashionable technology stock, and demand from investors who wanted the popular name pushed its price far above the value implied by 3Com's ownership stake. Marisol's model showed a large spread between the two securities. The apparent profit seemed almost riskless - until she examined whether she could actually execute both sides.

The short side created the first obstacle. Borrowing Palm shares was difficult and expensive because many traders wanted to short the same stock, while others wanted to own it for reasons unrelated to its underlying value. Even if Marisol secured the borrow, she could not know exactly when 3Com would distribute Palm shares or when the corporate separation would remove the pricing gap. Her capital could remain tied up while financing costs accumulated.

The trade also faced a practical danger: the price could move further away before it corrected. If Palm rose sharply, the short position could trigger margin calls even though the underlying relationship still looked wrong. Marisol therefore faced a real choice between recognizing a mispricing and surviving the period before the market corrected it. The gap persisted for months, demonstrating the central fact of arbitrage: a price can be wrong longer than a trader can remain funded.

How Marisol Tested the Constraint Stack

Marisol began by separating the trade's theoretical value from its executable value. She calculated the value of 3Com's Palm stake, then subtracted 3Com's debt and assigned a conservative value to its operating businesses. That exercise established the potential spread, but it did not establish a usable trade. She next listed every condition required for the spread to close:

- She needed to borrow Palm shares. - She needed enough borrowing capacity to maintain the short. - She needed a reliable estimate of the distribution timeline. - She needed cash to meet margin calls if Palm rose. - She needed a return large enough to cover borrow fees, financing costs, taxes, and delay.

This checklist formed the practical version of the **Shleifer-Vishny Constraint Stack**. The stack treats arbitrage as a chain of conditions rather than a single valuation judgment. A trade fails when any important layer breaks: mispricing identification, position construction, financing, timing, or risk control.

She then stress-tested the position. Instead of asking only what she would earn if Palm converged toward fair value, she asked what would happen if Palm rose another 20 percent before correction. A short position loses money as the borrowed asset rises. The broker can demand additional collateral, and the trader may need to close the position at the worst possible moment. Marisol sized the position around that interim risk, not around the final expected profit.

The next turning point came when she checked the share borrow. The quoted fee looked manageable for a short holding period, but the position had no dependable end date. A fee that seems minor over several weeks can consume much of the expected spread over several months. Worse, the lender could recall the shares. That would force Marisol to cover the short before the corporate event resolved the mispricing.

She also examined the source of demand for Palm. Some buyers did not care about the relationship between Palm and 3Com. They wanted exposure to a highly visible technology company, or they faced portfolio rules that favored the stock. Their demand could continue even when fundamental analysis showed an extreme valuation. Marisol treated this demand as a risk factor, not as evidence that the market would soon become rational.

The same logic applies beyond the 3Com-Palm case. During the August 2007 quantitative trading crisis, many funds held similar value, momentum, and mean-reversion positions. When several funds began selling at once, the same stocks moved against many strategies simultaneously. Losses triggered margin calls, and margin calls forced more selling. Arbitrage capital disappeared when the spreads became largest.

Relative-value trades faced similar pressure during the 2008 financial crisis. Convertible-bond traders and other spread-focused investors depended on financing from banks and brokerages. When those firms reduced lending and demanded more collateral, traders sold positions that might eventually have recovered. In March 2020,

Treasury cash-futures basis trades also came under pressure as investors rushed for cash. The instruments had a close economic relationship, but funding needs overwhelmed the ability of traders to maintain the position.

Marisol's final decision was not to reject arbitrage. She rejected the idea that a large spread automatically justified a large position. She recorded the theoretical spread, the expected holding period, the borrow terms, the maximum tolerable adverse move, and the amount of liquid cash available for margin. If any assumption lacked a dependable answer, she reduced the position or waited.

That process changed her definition of opportunity. A mispricing became investable only when she could explain not just why it should close, but why she could hold the trade until it closed. The distinction protected her from confusing a correct valuation with a safe transaction.

What the Constraint Stack Lets You Steal

A mispricing is not a trade until you can finance the wait. Start with a written convergence estimate and a maximum holding period. If your expected spread equals $10 per share but borrow, financing, and execution costs could consume $3, calculate the return on the capital actually tied up - not the headline spread. Then ask whether you can fund the position if the correction takes twice as long as expected. This matters because time converts a paper opportunity into a cash requirement.

Treat short selling as a separate risk, not the mirror image of buying. A long position can lose only the amount invested, but a short position can create rising collateral demands as the asset price increases. Before shorting, check the borrow fee, recall terms, available shares, and broker margin rules. Stress-test a 20 percent and 40 percent adverse move, even when your valuation says the asset looks expensive. Palm's price could rise while Palm remained overvalued; that interim move could force an otherwise correct trade to close.

Separate convergence risk from funding risk. Convergence risk asks whether the price relationship will correct. Funding risk asks whether you can keep the position open until that happens. Maintain a simple trade sheet with five lines: entry prices, expected exit condition, estimated time to exit, collateral requirement, and liquid cash reserve. Review the sheet whenever prices move sharply or financing terms change. A trade with attractive convergence but weak funding can damage your finances before the thesis receives a fair test.

Assume other investors may face the same exit at the same time. Crowded strategies can turn small price movements into forced liquidation. Look for shared exposures: the same sectors, factors, financing sources, or short positions. During the August 2007 quant crisis, similar models sold similar securities, so diversification by fund name did not create true diversification. For a personal portfolio, check whether several positions depend on the same market condition, such as low volatility, easy credit, or continued demand for growth stocks.

Demand a catalyst, but discount its timing. A catalyst is an event that can close the price gap, such as a merger, distribution, debt repayment, or contract settlement. Record the event date only when the process has a firm timetable; otherwise, use a range and size the trade for the longer end. In the 3Com-Palm situation, the corporate separation offered a path toward correction, but uncertainty about timing allowed the mispricing to persist. A catalyst improves the case; it does not remove the need for liquidity and patience.

The Shleifer-Vishny Constraint Stack turns arbitrage from a valuation exercise into a survival test. First identify the gap. Then test the position's construction, financing, timing, crowding, and worst interim outcome. Only after those layers hold together should you decide how much capital the opportunity deserves. Markets do not require every participant to be irrational; they only require enough practical constraints to prevent rational traders from correcting prices immediately. Understanding those constraints helps you distinguish a genuine opportunity from a spread that merely advertises its danger.

CHAPTER 31

Concrete Arbitrage Failures: LTCM Lessons

The Choice Between a Wide Spread and a Fragile Trade

What would you do if a trade looked almost certain to converge, yet the market moved against you long enough to threaten your account? That question defines the lesson of Long-Term Capital Management (LTCM). The fund did not fail because its managers misunderstood every price relationship. It failed because a reasonable convergence trade met three forces at once: noise-trader risk, capital withdrawal, and funding liquidity pressure.

LTCM often bought securities that appeared cheap and sold related securities that appeared expensive. The trade depended on the prices moving together again. In calm markets, the spread could narrow while the fund earned a modest return. In stressed markets, however, investors sold what they could, lenders reduced financing, and other firms unwound similar positions. Prices moved farther apart precisely when the trade required patience and cash.

Dante, a 50-year-old risk officer, would describe the decision in practical terms: a spread is not an opportunity until you can survive its maximum plausible widening. If you buy a cheap bond and short an expensive related bond, you do not control when convergence occurs. You control only the position size, the financing terms, the collateral you hold, and the point at which you exit. Choose incorrectly, and a trade that eventually proves "right" can still produce a permanent loss before convergence arrives.

The LTCM Failure Chain makes this sequence visible:

apparent mispricing → crowded trade → noise-driven divergence → margin pressure → capital withdrawal → forced selling → wider mispricing.

The chain matters because each link strengthens the next. A falling price creates a margin call. The margin call forces a sale. The sale pushes the price lower. A lender then sees greater risk and demands more collateral. The original trade becomes even harder to hold.

Comparing Ways to Handle Convergence Risk

Before entering a convergence trade, choose how much exposure you want to take and how much of the trade you want to leave unfinanced. The following approaches address the same problem in different ways.

Approach	Cost	Time to manage	Difficulty	Best for
Fully funded relative-value trade	High capital requirement; low borrowing cost	Moderate	Moderate	Investors who can hold through long delays
Small leveraged convergence trade	Lower upfront capital; financing and margin costs apply	High; requires frequent checks	High	Experienced traders with reliable financing
Paired exposure with a defined exit	Moderate capital requirement; possible trading costs	Moderate	Moderate	Investors who need a clear loss limit

A fully funded trade removes the most dangerous part of the LTCM Failure Chain: the lender's forced timetable. If you buy one bond and sell a related bond without borrowing heavily against the position, a temporary price gap does not automatically create a margin call. You still face noise-trader risk, because prices can diverge, but you gain time. Time does not guarantee convergence; it simply prevents a lender from deciding the outcome before the market does.

A small leveraged trade can improve the return on your capital, but it adds a second price to monitor: the cost and availability of funding. A broker may change margin requirements while the underlying relationship remains intact. A defined exit offers more discipline, but it cannot guarantee execution at the planned price during a disorderly market. Dante's practical distinction is simple: an exit rule limits your decision-making risk, while cash reserves limit your funding risk. You need both.

The 3Com and Palm episode shows why "related" does not mean "safe." When 3Com announced that it would distribute Palm shares, Palm traded at a price that implied a negative value for 3Com's remaining businesses. The apparent arbitrage involved buying 3Com and shorting Palm. Yet short-sale restrictions, uncertainty about the distribution, and strong demand for the fashionable technology stock delayed convergence. The relationship looked mechanical, but the trade still depended on timing, borrow availability, and investor behavior.

The Verdict: Survive First, Converge Second

For a beginner, choose a fully funded or very lightly financed relative-value trade, and keep the position small enough to withstand a prolonged divergence. This approach costs more capital, but it directly addresses the failure mechanism that destroyed LTCM. A trade that earns a small spread cannot justify a structure that can force you out at a large loss.

If you have professional trading experience, stable financing, and daily access to margin information, a small leveraged trade may fit - but only after you calculate the effect of wider spreads and higher collateral demands. Do not rely on the historical relationship alone. Test what happens if the spread doubles, triples, or moves beyond every observation in your available history.

If you cannot explain the borrow terms, collateral rules, exit price, and maximum cash requirement in plain language, do not enter the trade. Complexity does not create protection. It often hides the point at which a lender or counterparty can change the rules.

Use this decision flowchart:

If you cannot fund the position without depending on daily borrowing, choose a fully funded trade or avoid it. If the trade requires shorting an asset with uncertain borrow availability, choose a different pair. If you can fund the position, monitor it daily, and define a loss limit before entry, choose a small position. If a spread widens while financing costs or margin requirements rise, reduce exposure rather than adding automatically. If several related trades begin moving against you at the same time, assume crowding and capital withdrawal may be active, and exit before forced selling makes the decision for you.

The central recommendation follows the LTCM Failure Chain: size the trade for the funding crisis, not the calm-market spread. A narrow historical spread may tempt you to use leverage. A stress-tested position tells you whether you can remain solvent when noise traders, lenders, and other arbitrageurs all act against you.

Making the LTCM Failure Chain Practical

1. **Write down the exact convergence claim.** State why the two assets should move together. For example, do not write "these bonds look mispriced." Write, "The price difference should narrow because both bonds represent claims on the same issuer, have comparable maturity, and receive the same recovery treatment." List every condition that must remain true. If the trade depends on a merger, distribution, conversion, or legal approval, identify the date and the risk of delay.

2. **Measure the spread in money, not only in percentages.** Record the current price difference, the normal range, and the loss produced by a wider gap. If a pair normally differs by $2 and your position loses $10,000 for every additional dollar of divergence, calculate the cash loss at gaps of $4, $6, and $10. This exercise exposes whether the trade can survive ordinary stress.

3. **Model noise-trader risk separately.** Ask what happens if investors buy the expensive asset because it is popular, liquid, or easy to discuss. The Palm example shows how demand for a fashionable security can overpower a fundamental relationship. Identify which side of your trade attracts momentum buyers and assume that side can become more expensive before it becomes cheaper.

4. **Confirm the short position before committing capital.** Check the borrow rate, recall terms, available shares, and the broker's right to increase margin. A short position can fail even when your valuation is correct if the lender recalls the shares or raises the collateral requirement. Save the terms in writing and review them whenever the position changes.

5. **Calculate the funding requirement under stress.** Include the initial collateral, daily variation losses, financing costs, and an

additional cash reserve. Test a scenario in which both legs move against you temporarily. Then test a worse scenario in which the broker raises the margin requirement while the spread widens. If the required cash exceeds what you can provide without selling unrelated assets, reduce the position.

6. **Check for crowding and correlated exposure.** List other positions that depend on the same market condition. Several apparently different trades may all require tight credit spreads, stable volatility, or available short borrow. During the August 2007 quant crisis, many strategies sold similar stocks at the same time. Treat shared exposure as one position, not as separate sources of diversification.

7. **Set an exit rule before the market moves.** Define a price level, cash loss, financing change, or thesis failure that ends the trade. A spread widening alone does not always disprove convergence, but a margin increase, borrow recall, or change in the legal structure may destroy the original thesis. Write down which event requires immediate action and which event permits continued holding.

8. **Review the position on a fixed schedule.** Check market prices, financing terms, collateral, borrow availability, and the original convergence conditions at least daily for leveraged trades. Record the result. A written log prevents you from replacing analysis with hope after a loss.

Act today:

- Choose one proposed convergence trade and write its exact economic link. - Calculate the cash loss if the spread reaches two wider stress levels. - Obtain the broker's current borrow and margin terms in writing. - Identify every other holding exposed to the same funding or market factor. - Set the exit condition before placing the order.

LTCM's failure did not prove that convergence trading never works. It proved that convergence cannot protect a position that lacks time, cash, or independent financing. The durable lesson reaches beyond hedge funds: when money and credit tighten, the market can remain wrong longer than a leveraged investor can remain solvent. Build every trade around that fact, and arbitrage becomes a measured risk rather than a promise of easy correction.

CHAPTER 32

Western Asset Cherry-Picking: Allocation Fraud

When Filled Trades Become Fiduciary Harm

A trade can fill in seconds, yet an investment account may wait hours - or days - for its final allocation. That timing gap creates a serious control risk: the manager can see the execution price before deciding which client receives which portion. The conduct may involve no market manipulation, false order, or insider information. The harm can arise solely from choosing recipients after the result becomes known.

This risk matters most when several accounts receive different prices, partial fills, or allocations across securities with unequal liquidity. Claire, a 38-year-old fixed-income operations lead, may process a block order for several portfolios and discover that one bond tranche performed better than another. If she assigns the better result after the fill, she has changed the economic outcome for clients using information created by the trade itself.

The **Allocation-Timing Red Flag** gives investors, trustees, and operations staff a practical test. Record the intended allocation before execution, preserve the trade and allocation timestamps, compare the final distribution with the original plan, and investigate every material change. The goal is not to accuse someone of manipulation. The goal is to prevent discretionary timing from becoming an undisclosed transfer of value between fiduciary accounts.

Your Toolkit for Proving Allocation Timing

- **Pre-trade allocation schedule** - List each account, target amount, security, and allocation method before sending the order. Use the firm's order-management system or a controlled spreadsheet with a locked timestamp; basic spreadsheet software costs little, while an order-management system usually comes through the firm's existing broker or custodian.

- **Execution blotter** - Capture order submission, partial fills, cancellations, and final execution times. Request it from the broker, custodian, or trading platform; most regulated investment operations already receive this record as part of normal trade reporting.

- **Allocation ledger** - Record the exact quantity and price assigned to each account, including commissions, accrued interest, and fees. Build it in a read-only file or accounting system so later edits leave an audit trail.

- **Time-synchronized records** - Compare clocks across the trading system, allocation system, email server, and custodian. Use the firm's approved time source and document any clock difference; a timestamp that appears earlier on one system may occur later in real time.

- **Exception log** - Record every departure from the original allocation, its reason, approver, and supporting evidence. A simple controlled log costs nothing beyond staff time, but it prevents "the market changed" from becoming an unsupported explanation.

- **Independent review sample** - Select completed blocks and compare planned allocations with final allocations. An internal compliance team, outside reviewer, or trustee can perform the check;

the important feature is independence from the person who made the allocation.

- **Client fairness worksheet** - Recalculate what each account received compared with the available fill. Include average price, quantity, accrued interest, and expenses. This worksheet reveals whether a change improved one account while leaving another with an inferior result.

The tools work together. A pre-trade schedule shows intent. The execution blotter shows what became available. The allocation ledger shows who received it. The exception log explains any change. Without all four, a reviewer may see a suspicious outcome but lack the timing evidence needed to distinguish a clerical error from a discretionary decision.

The Allocation-Timing Red Flag: Action Plan

1. **Freeze the intended allocation before order release.** Enter each account's target quantity or percentage before the trader submits the block order. Lock the file or system record. The specific outcome is a time-stamped plan that exists before anyone knows the execution result.

2. **Define the allocation rule in plain language.** State whether the firm will allocate pro rata, use round lots, follow account-specific limits, or apply another documented method. For example, if three accounts each seek 100 bonds and the order fills only 180, write the rule that determines how those 180 bonds will be divided.

3. **Capture every execution event.** Preserve the time, quantity, price, venue, and security for each fill. A fixed-income order may fill across several dealers or tranches, so do not rely only on the final

average price. The outcome should show exactly what inventory became available and when.

4. **Compare the fill with account eligibility.** Remove accounts that could not legally or prudently receive the security because of mandate restrictions, minimum denominations, liquidity limits, tax status, or concentration rules. Record the reason for each exclusion before allocation. This prevents legitimate eligibility changes from looking like preference for a favored account.

5. **Apply the pre-set rule immediately after the fill.** Allocate the available security using the recorded method, not the price performance that appears after execution. If the block contains several prices, apply the same method across the relevant fills unless the policy clearly requires another approach.

6. **Create an exception before changing the allocation.** If the original plan cannot work, stop and document the problem before assigning the better or worse fill. Identify the failed assumption, the proposed replacement rule, the affected accounts, and the approving person. The specific outcome is a contemporaneous explanation rather than a justification written after a complaint.

7. **Separate trading authority from allocation approval.** Have a second person review material changes, especially when the change benefits an account connected to the manager, a fee arrangement, a performance target, or a senior relationship. Claire should not approve her own exception when the exception changes which client receives the better execution.

8. **Run a client-by-client fairness calculation.** Compare each account's final quantity and average price with the result it would have received under the pre-trade rule. Include accrued interest in bond

trades because a lower clean price does not necessarily mean a lower total cost. Flag any account that lost value because another account received a more favorable fill.

9. **Review the timing, not only the result.** Ask whether the allocation decision occurred before the relevant execution, after the execution, or after the manager could observe which securities or prices looked attractive. A fair-looking final split can still conceal a weak process; a changed split can also be legitimate if the records show a real eligibility or settlement problem.

10. **Escalate repeated exceptions.** Set a written threshold, such as any unexplained change affecting two or more accounts or any change that improves one account at another's expense. Send those cases to compliance, the investment committee, trustee, or governing body. Repetition matters because a pattern can reveal a control failure even when each individual explanation sounds plausible.

11. **Notify affected clients when required.** If a material allocation error occurred, follow the firm's correction, reimbursement, and disclosure procedures. Do not quietly reverse the trade without preserving the original records. A correction repairs the account; it does not erase the decision history.

12. **Test the control on closed trades.** Each month, select a sample of completed blocks and reconstruct the timeline from the original order through settlement. Check the pre-trade plan, fills, allocation, exceptions, approvals, and client impact. A control works only when an independent reviewer can reproduce the result without asking the original decision-maker to explain missing records.

Consider Claire's fixed-income block order. Three portfolios requested the same corporate bond. Before release, she records equal target quantities. The order fills partly in a more attractive tranche and partly in a less attractive tranche. After seeing the fills, she assigns the attractive tranche to the portfolio with the strongest recent performance and distributes the less attractive tranche to the other two. She never placed a false order or moved the market. Nevertheless, she used post-fill knowledge to alter the economic result.

The correct response does not depend on proving bad intent. The records should show whether the tranche allocation followed a pre-existing rule, reflected account eligibility, or changed after Claire could identify the better result. If she had documented a rule requiring pro rata distribution by fill and applied it consistently, the process would remain reviewable. If she changed the split without a recorded reason, the Allocation-Timing Red Flag has activated.

Quick Reference for Allocation Reviews

Red flag - The final allocation differs from the pre-trade plan after the manager can see prices, fills, or security performance.

Strong control - The firm records the allocation before order release, locks the record, and applies the same rule to all eligible accounts.

Required timestamps - Order entry, order release, each fill, allocation decision, exception approval, and settlement instruction.

If a fill is partial - Apply the documented partial-fill rule; do not give the scarce quantity to the account that appears most attractive after execution.

If a security has multiple tranches - Record the tranche, price, quantity, and eligibility for each account. Do not treat unequal tranches as interchangeable without a written basis.

If an account becomes ineligible - Document the restriction before reallocating its portion and preserve the evidence.

If one account benefits and another loses - Require independent review and calculate the value difference, including interest and expenses.

If records appear inconsistent - Reconcile system clocks and obtain source records from the broker or custodian before drawing conclusions.

If the exception repeats - Escalate the pattern. Repeated "one-off" changes indicate a process problem or a conflict that the firm has failed to control.

If the allocation cannot be reconstructed - Treat the missing evidence as a control deficiency, not as proof that the allocation was fair.

Core question - Did the decision follow a rule established before the fill, or did someone use the fill to decide who received the better result?

A market can remain orderly while fiduciary harm occurs inside the account-allocation process. The essential protection is temporal: decide the rule before knowledge of the result, preserve the evidence, and review every departure. That discipline connects modern asset management to the older mechanics of exchange: value must move according to an understood rule, not according to whoever gains information first.

CHAPTER 33

Treasury Basis Trades and Stress Amplification

Why a Treasury Basis Trade Can Become a Liquidity Problem

A Treasury futures spread can look almost riskless on a calm trading desk: buy a Treasury bond, sell a futures contract, and wait for the prices to converge. Then funding costs rise, margin calls arrive, and the supposedly small spread loss forces a large sale of an otherwise liquid asset. The trade does not fail because the bond suddenly becomes worthless. It fails because the financing structure cannot survive the timing of the loss.

That distinction matters for anyone building wealth through bonds, funds, or macro-sensitive assets. A cash-futures basis trade links three moving parts: the Treasury price, the futures price, and the money used to hold the position. A trader who watches only the spread can miss the most important risk - the need to produce cash before convergence occurs.

The Basis-and-Bridge Stress Model gives you a practical way to examine that risk. You will learn how the trade works, how leverage magnifies small price moves, how margin and borrowing costs create forced selling, and how to test whether a position can survive a rough period without relying on perfect market access.

How the Basis-and-Bridge Stress Model Works

The **basis** measures the relationship between the cash Treasury and the comparable futures contract. A trader may buy a Treasury bond at $100.00 and sell a futures contract at a price that implies $100.40 for the same economic exposure. The apparent spread equals $0.40, but that number does not represent a guaranteed profit. The trader must adjust for the bond's coupon, the cost of financing, the futures contract's delivery rules, and the exact Treasury that can satisfy delivery.

The **bridge** means the funding and collateral structure that carries the trade from entry to convergence. A trader borrows against the Treasury, posts margin on the futures position, and expects the price relationship to narrow over time. If the lender increases the required collateral or the futures exchange demands more margin, the bridge requires additional cash. The trade can then produce a cash loss even when its long-term economics remain intact.

Use the Basis-and-Bridge Stress Model through four checks:

1. **Measure the true basis.** Compare the cash bond and futures price after accounting for the coupon, accrued interest, conversion factor, delivery month, and expected financing cost. A quoted spread without these adjustments can create a false sense of safety.

2. **Map the bridge.** Record the purchase price, borrowed amount, interest rate, initial margin, variation margin, collateral haircut, and available cash. This step shows how much liquidity the position needs before convergence.

3. **Stress the path, not only the destination.** Test what happens if the basis widens before it narrows. A position may show a positive expected return at maturity but still fail after a temporary adverse move. Include higher borrowing costs, larger margin requirements, and a decline in the value of the Treasury collateral.

4. **Set a survival limit.** Decide the maximum cash call and maximum basis widening the trade can withstand. Close or reduce the position before the bridge breaks, not after the lender or clearing broker makes that decision.

Leverage turns a narrow spread into a large account movement. Suppose Samir buys $100 million of Treasuries with $5 million of his own capital and borrows the remaining $95 million. A price decline of only $0.50 per $100 of face value reduces the bond position by $500,000. That move consumes 10 percent of his equity before fees, financing, or futures margin. If the basis widens by another $0.50, the loss can become material even though the trade still appears likely to converge later.

A futures position also creates daily cash settlement. When the short futures contract loses value, Samir must pay variation margin promptly. The cash bond may recover later, but the futures loss arrives first. This timing mismatch explains why a trade can remain economically attractive and still trigger liquidation.

Putting the Model Into Practice

Samir, a 45-year-old macro trader, identifies a cash-futures basis that appears to offer a $0.30 gain per $100 of Treasury exposure after estimated coupon and financing adjustments. He plans to buy $20 million of the cash Treasury and sell the matching futures exposure. He contributes $1.5 million of capital and finances the rest.

1. **Calculate the starting position.** Samir buys $20 million of Treasuries and borrows $18.5 million. His initial equity equals $1.5 million. If the expected net convergence equals $0.30 per $100, the gross expected gain equals $60,000 before execution costs and financing changes.

2. **Record the daily cash obligations.** He lists the futures margin requirement, the lender's collateral haircut, the interest rate on the borrowing, and the cash held outside the trade. He keeps $600,000 available for margin and collateral calls rather than treating every dollar as investable capital.

3. **Apply a basis-widening test.** Samir tests a widening of $0.75 per $100. On $20 million, that movement represents a $150,000 relative-value loss before other effects. He then tests a $1.50 widening, which represents $300,000. The purpose is not to predict the exact move; it is to identify whether the account can fund the position through an uncomfortable but plausible dislocation.

4. **Add the funding shock.** He assumes the borrowing rate rises by 2 percentage points and the lender raises the required collateral. If the additional collateral exceeds his available cash, he reduces the trade immediately. The expected $60,000 convergence gain cannot justify a structure that may force a sale at a much larger loss.

5. **Set the exit rule.** Samir chooses a maximum basis widening of $1.25 and a maximum cash call of $400,000. If either threshold occurs, he closes part of the position. He does not wait for a forecast to improve because the decision concerns liquidity, not direction.

6. **Reconcile the result.** If the basis narrows as expected, Samir calculates the actual result after borrowing interest, futures fees, bid-ask spreads, and taxes. If the trade loses money, he identifies whether the cause came from the basis, financing, delivery assumptions, or forced timing. That record improves the next risk estimate.

Quick checklist

- Match the cash Treasury with the correct futures contract and delivery month. - Include coupon income, accrued interest, conversion factors, and financing costs. - Calculate the dollar loss from each $0.25 or $0.50 basis movement. - Separate cash held for margin from cash available for new investments. - Test higher borrowing rates and larger collateral requirements. - Check whether a lender can demand repayment or additional collateral. - Set a maximum cash call before entering the position. - Reduce exposure when the trade approaches that limit. - Track futures settlement cash separately from the bond's market value. - Recalculate the trade after every major funding or margin change.

This process also applies indirectly to investors. A highly leveraged relative-value fund may hold Treasury basis trades through a brokerage or pooled vehicle. The investor may not see the individual futures contracts, but the fund's liquidation risk can still affect returns. A fund that sells Treasuries to meet margin calls can add pressure to the same market that other funds are trying to exit.

Mistakes and Edge Cases That Break the Bridge

Mistaking convergence for a guaranteed profit

The cash Treasury and futures contract may not converge exactly as a simple price chart suggests. Delivery options, the cheapest-to-deliver bond, coupon timing, and financing assumptions can change the result.

Do this: calculate the basis using the actual deliverable bond, conversion factor, accrued interest, coupon dates, and expected financing period.

Not this: subtract the two quoted prices and treat the difference as locked-in income.

Using too much leverage

Leverage makes a small relative-value spread look attractive because the position controls more assets with less capital. It also makes a temporary loss consume equity quickly. A $0.50 adverse move on $100 million represents $500,000, regardless of whether the expected final spread equals only a few cents.

Do this: express every stress move in dollars and compare it with both equity and immediately available cash.

Not this: judge risk by the percentage size of the spread alone.

Ignoring the funding clock

A trader may have enough total wealth to hold a position but not enough cash to satisfy today's margin call. The market can force a sale before the expected convergence arrives. March 2020 showed how even the U.S. Treasury market can experience severe pressure when investors simultaneously seek cash and reduce leveraged positions.

Do this: maintain a dated cash-flow schedule showing when futures settlement, interest, collateral calls, and debt repayment can occur.

Not this: assume that a liquid Treasury can always sell at a stable price when the entire market seeks liquidity.

Treating liquidity as constant

Bid-ask spreads can widen, dealer balance sheets can shrink, and execution size can move the market. A position that looks easy to close in ordinary conditions may require several transactions during stress.

Do this: test exits at smaller trade sizes and use conservative execution prices.

Not this: base the exit plan on the last quoted price during calm trading.

The central lesson is precise: the basis describes the price relationship, while the bridge determines whether the trader can remain in the position long enough for that relationship to matter. Barter, credit, and modern money all depend on settlement timing and trust. Treasury basis trades add a highly financial version of the same problem. The asset may retain value, yet the obligation to settle today can overwhelm the ability to wait. A sound trade therefore requires more than a favorable spread. It requires enough cash, collateral, and time to cross the bridge

BONUS CHAPTER

Beyond Barter: The Architecture of Value

The most important question in this book is not whether barter came before money.

It is not even whether money emerged because barter was inconvenient.

Those questions matter, but they are narrower than the larger problem.

The deeper question is:

How do human beings make value transferable?

That question connects every chapter of this book.

Barter attempts to transfer value directly.

Credit transfers value through time.

Reciprocity transfers value through relationships.

Money transfers value through general acceptance.

Markets transfer value through prices.

Assets transfer claims on future value.

Different systems solve different versions of the same fundamental problem.

1. Value Is Not the Same as Price

One of the easiest mistakes in economics is to treat price and value as identical.

They are not.

A bottle of water may have a low market price in a supermarket and extraordinary practical value to a person stranded without water.

A piece of equipment may have a high advertised price but little value to a buyer who has no use for it.

The manuscript repeatedly demonstrates this distinction through barter examples. A quoted retail price does not automatically equal the value received by the other party.

Barter, Money, And Market Mechanics.docx

This distinction is essential.

Price is a measurement produced by an exchange system.

Value is the usefulness, desirability, scarcity, security, income, or other benefit attributed to something.

The two interact, but they are not identical.

That is why barter requires reference prices without becoming identical to a cash transaction.

When Leila evaluates a website, she does not merely ask what the designer normally charges. She asks what the website is worth **to her** under realistic alternatives.

This is a profound economic principle.

The market price may tell you what something commonly sells for.

It does not necessarily tell you what it is worth to you.

2. The Five Layers of Exchange

A useful way to understand any exchange is to separate five layers.

Layer One: The Asset

What is actually being transferred?

It may be:

- a physical product;
- labor;
- expertise;
- access;
- a service;
- a financial claim;
- a future promise;
- information;
- or a combination.

A barter exchange might transfer goods.

A credit exchange transfers goods now against a promise later.

A financial market may transfer a claim on future income.

The first question is therefore:

What exactly changes hands?

Layer Two: Measurement

How do participants measure the thing?

A service may be measured in hours.

A commodity may be measured by weight.

A product may be measured by units.

A financial asset may be measured in dollars.

Without measurement, comparison becomes difficult.

This is why the manuscript repeatedly emphasizes reference values, quantities, dates, and records.

A transaction becomes easier to manage when participants can answer:

How much?

Layer Three: Acceptance

Measurement alone is insufficient.

An asset may have value but fail as a means of payment.

A person may own a valuable cow but be unable to use it to pay for a $20 meal.

A commodity may be desirable but inconvenient to transport.

A financial instrument may be valuable but unacceptable to a particular seller.

This is the difference between **value** and **liquidity**.

Liquidity concerns how easily something can be converted into an accepted form of purchasing power.

The manuscript's discussion of proto-money already approaches this insight by distinguishing something valuable from something that performs monetary functions.

Barter, Money, And Market Mechanics.docx

3. Trust Is the Invisible Infrastructure

Every exchange system requires trust.

Barter requires trust that the other person will deliver.

Credit requires trust that the future obligation will be honored.

Money requires trust that others will accept it.

Markets require trust in contracts, institutions, records, and settlement systems.

Even electronic money depends on infrastructure that participants believe will continue operating.

Trust does not mean blind faith.

It can be supported by:

- reputation;
- contracts;
- collateral;
- law;
- accounting;
- repeated interaction;
- institutional enforcement;
- technological verification.

This explains why records are so important throughout the manuscript.

A record transforms memory into an institutional claim.

The ancient tablet and the modern digital ledger are separated by thousands of years, but they solve a related problem:

Who owes what to whom?

The manuscript's credit-first framework makes this point particularly clearly.

Barter, Money, And Market Mechanics.docx

4. Time Changes Value

A second major insight is that value exists across time.

A $1,000 payment today is not necessarily equivalent to a $1,000 promise next year.

Why?

Because waiting creates risk.

The recipient may need cash now.

The promised value may change.

The other party may fail.

Prices may move.

Opportunities may disappear.

This is why credit is fundamentally different from barter.

Barter attempts to settle immediately.

Credit allows settlement across time.

That flexibility creates enormous economic power---but also risk.

A promise is an asset to one party and a liability to another.

The same transaction therefore creates two perspectives.

The person waiting for payment sees a receivable.

The person who must pay sees an obligation.

The architecture of markets depends heavily on managing these opposing claims.

5. Money Is a Bridge

Money can therefore be understood as a bridge.

It bridges:

different wants,

different locations,

different times,

different quantities,

and sometimes

different levels of trust.

Suppose you provide $500 worth of services to someone who does not possess anything you currently need.

Barter asks:

"Can this person give me something I want?"

Money asks:

"Can this person give me something other people will accept?"

That is a tremendous expansion of the possible trading network.

Instead of searching for one perfect trading partner, you can sell to one person and buy from another.

The manuscript's discussion of the double-coincidence problem demonstrates exactly why this separation allows markets to expand.

Barter, Money, And Market Mechanics.docx

Money therefore does not eliminate value.

It **separates the act of selling from the act of buying.**

That may be one of its most important economic functions.

6. But Money Does Not Eliminate Barter

If money is so efficient, why does barter keep returning?

Because no exchange system solves every problem.

When cash becomes scarce, businesses may trade.

When credit becomes difficult, companies may accept goods.

When currencies become unreliable, people may use alternative assets.

When communities want to mobilize unused skills, they may use time banks.

The manuscript's later chapters demonstrate precisely this adaptability. Countertrade, time banks, peer-to-peer exchange, and barter networks all represent alternative mechanisms for moving value.

Barter, Money, And Market Mechanics.docx

The lesson is not that one system defeats another.

The lesson is that humans use **multiple settlement mechanisms simultaneously**.

A modern business might use:

- cash for payroll;

- credit for suppliers;
- barter for selected services;
- inventory as collateral;
- financial assets for investment;
- and contractual claims for future revenue.

The economy is therefore not one system.

It is an ecosystem of systems.

7. Liquidity Is the Hidden Question

Consider two assets.

Asset A is worth $100,000 but takes six months to sell.

Asset B is worth $95,000 and can be sold tomorrow.

Which is more useful to someone facing an emergency?

The answer may be Asset B.

This is why market mechanics cannot be understood through price alone.

We must ask:

Can the value be accessed when needed?

That is liquidity.

Liquidity explains why people sometimes accept a lower price for immediate cash.

It also explains why certain forms of money become powerful.

A widely accepted currency may be less intrinsically useful than a commodity, but it may be dramatically easier to transfer.

The market therefore rewards not only value but **convertibility**.

8. The Three Questions Every Exchange Should Answer

After studying barter, credit, money, and markets, we can reduce the entire subject to three questions.

Question One:

What is being transferred?

Identify the actual asset.

Question Two:

What makes the recipient willing to accept it?

Identify usefulness, scarcity, price, reputation, legal enforceability, network acceptance, or expected future exchangeability.

Question Three:

How does the recipient convert it into what they ultimately need?

This final question is often overlooked.

A seller may accept an asset only because they believe someone else will accept it.

That creates a chain.

The chain can be short:

Goods → Money → Goods

Or complicated:

Labor → Credit → Service → Commodity → Cash

The longer the chain becomes, the more important trust, records, standards, and institutions become.

9. The Market Is a Network, Not a Marketplace

The word "market" often creates a mental image of a physical location.

But markets are better understood as networks.

A market connects:

- buyers;
- sellers;
- lenders;
- borrowers;
- intermediaries;
- institutions;
- payment systems;
- information systems;
- regulators;
- and settlement mechanisms.

Barter creates relatively small networks because participants must find compatible wants.

Money expands the network.

Credit expands it across time.

Institutions expand it across distance.

Technology expands it across geography.

Modern markets therefore represent an enormous evolution of the same underlying challenge:

How can value move safely between people who do not know each other, do not want the same things, and may never meet?

10. The Wealth Lesson

This brings the discussion back to wealth.

Wealth is often confused with possession.

But possession alone is insufficient.

A person may own an asset that cannot be sold.

A business may report profits but have no cash.

An investor may own a valuable property but struggle to access funds.

A company may possess inventory but lack buyers.

A community may possess enormous human skills but lack a mechanism for coordinating them.

The deeper lesson is:

Economic power comes not merely from possessing value, but from being able to mobilize value.

That is why liquidity, trust, networks, contracts, information, and reputation matter.

The person who understands these mechanisms sees beyond price.

They see the machinery beneath the price.

11. The Complete Architecture

We can now assemble the entire argument of this book.

Barter solves direct exchange.

Credit solves exchange across time.

Reciprocity solves exchange through relationships.

Money solves exchange across mismatched wants.

Accounting measures obligations.

Contracts formalize expectations.

Markets connect independent participants.

Liquidity makes value transferable.

Institutions make exchange more predictable.

Technology expands the network.

And **trust** holds the entire architecture together.

This is why the history of money cannot be reduced to the story of coins.

Coins are only one visible expression of a much larger human invention:

the ability to make value portable across circumstances.

12. The Final Principle

If there is one principle worth carrying from this book into everyday life, it is this:

Never ask only what something is worth. Ask what makes that value transferable.

A product may be valuable.

A skill may be valuable.

A property may be valuable.

A promise may be valuable.

A currency may be valuable.

An investment may be valuable.

But value becomes economically powerful when it can be:

measured, trusted, transferred, accepted, and eventually converted into something useful.

That is the architecture behind markets.

That is the bridge between barter and money.

And that is why the study of ancient exchange remains relevant to modern wealth.

EPILOGUE

The Thing Behind the Thing

We began with a simple question:

Why did humans need money?

By now, the answer should feel less simple.

Money did not emerge into an empty world.

Human beings were already exchanging.

They were giving.

Borrowing.

Remembering.

Promising.

Sharing.

Trading.

Recording.

Redistributing.

Negotiating.

And trusting.

Barter was one part of this much larger landscape.

Its importance lies not in being the universal first stage of economic history, but in revealing one of the fundamental difficulties of exchange: **people rarely want exactly what one another has, at exactly the same time, in exactly the same quantity.**

Credit provided another answer.

Reciprocity provided another.

Gift exchange provided another.

Accounting provided another.

Money provided another.

Markets combined them.

The result is the extraordinary economic world in which we live.

A number on a screen can represent years of labor.

A piece of paper can represent purchasing power.

A signature can create an obligation.

A digital entry can transfer ownership.

A warehouse full of goods can become cash.

A promise can become an asset.

None of these things is magical.

They work because systems of measurement, acceptance, trust, law, institutions, expectations, and human behavior surround them.

That is the thing behind the thing.

And perhaps that is the most important lesson.

Money is not wealth itself.

Money is one of the mechanisms through which humans organize access to wealth.

Price is not value itself.

Price is one way a market communicates about value.

Possession is not liquidity.

An asset becomes more economically useful when its value can be mobilized.

And **markets are not merely places where things are bought and sold.**

They are systems through which strangers coordinate.

Once we see exchange this way, barter stops looking primitive.

Money stops looking mysterious.

Credit stops looking like merely borrowing.

And markets stop looking like machines operating independently of human beings.

They become what they have always been:

human inventions for solving the problem of value.

The forms will continue to change.

The currencies will change.

The technologies will change.

The assets will change.

But the fundamental problem will remain.

Someone will have something.

Someone else will need something.

And humanity will continue searching for the most reliable bridge between them.

Author's Note

This book began with a deceptively simple subject: barter.

The deeper investigation revealed that barter is only one doorway into a much larger subject---the mechanics through which human beings measure, transfer, preserve, and settle value.

The goal of this book is therefore not to offer a single simplistic origin story for money. It is to encourage readers to look beneath familiar economic labels and examine the actual mechanics of exchange.

Whenever possible, distinguish historical evidence from economic models, and distinguish both from interpretation.

That discipline is especially important when discussing the origins of money, because a logical explanation of why something would be useful does not automatically prove that history followed that exact sequence.

How to Read This Book

You can read this book in three ways.

As economic history: Follow the development of exchange from direct trade through credit, reciprocity, proto-money and monetary systems.

As a practical business book: Use the frameworks for evaluating barter, credit, countertrade, alternative exchange, and liquidity.

As a book about wealth: Look beyond prices and examine acceptance, trust, timing, risk, liquidity and convertibility.

The third approach may ultimately be the most important.

Key Concepts at a Glance

Barter

Direct exchange of goods or services without money serving as the intermediary.

Double Coincidence of Wants

The difficulty of finding another party who simultaneously wants what you offer and offers what you need.

Credit

A present transfer supported by an obligation to repay or return value later.

Reciprocity

A system in which value moves between participants without necessarily being exchanged simultaneously or identically.

Unit of Account

A common measure used to express and compare economic values.

Medium of Exchange

Something widely accepted for settling transactions.

Store of Value

Something that can preserve purchasing power or economic value across time, subject to risk.

Liquidity

The ease with which an asset can be converted into an accepted form of purchasing power.

Countertrade

A commercial arrangement in which a transaction includes reciprocal purchases, goods, credits, or other non-cash settlement mechanisms.

Time Bank

An organized exchange system in which participants earn and spend credits based primarily on time contributed.

A Practical Exchange Audit

Before accepting any barter, credit, countertrade, or alternative exchange arrangement, ask:

1. **What exactly am I receiving?**
2. **What exactly am I giving?**
3. **What is the realistic cash alternative?**
4. **When does each side deliver?**
5. **What happens if one side fails?**
6. **How liquid is what I receive?**
7. **Who else would accept it?**
8. **What records are required?**
9. **Are there tax or legal obligations?**
10. **Does the arrangement genuinely improve my position?**

The manuscript already emphasizes measurable deliverables, realistic cash alternatives, dates, remedies, records, and tax considerations.

Barter, Money, And Market Mechanics.docx

Final Reflection

The history of exchange teaches a surprisingly modern lesson.

Value is only useful when it can move.

A skill that nobody can access has limited economic power.

An asset nobody will accept has limited liquidity.

A promise nobody trusts has limited value.

A currency nobody accepts cannot function effectively as money.

A market without reliable settlement becomes fragile.

Economic systems therefore depend on more than production.

They depend on **conversion**.

Human beings create value, measure value, exchange value, store value, and attempt to transfer value across time.

Barter was one answer.

Credit was another.

Money became another.

Markets combined them.

And the search continues.

Acknowledgments

I am grateful to every reader who is willing to question familiar economic stories.

Some of the most important ideas begin with ordinary questions:

Why do people accept money?

Why does something become valuable?

Why does credit exist?

Why does barter return when cash becomes difficult?

Why can one asset be more useful than another even when its nominal price is lower?

Questions like these remind us that economics is not merely a collection of formulas.

It is the study of human behavior under conditions of scarcity, uncertainty, opportunity, trust, and choice.

I hope this book encourages readers to ask better questions about the economic systems surrounding them.

About the Author

Rupen O. Adhikari is an author whose work explores economics, philosophy, business, human behavior, success, markets, and the questions that connect everyday life with larger ideas.

His writing often begins with an apparently ordinary concept and examines the deeper mechanism beneath it.

In *Barter, Money, and Market Mechanics*, he explores exchange not merely as the movement of goods, but as one of humanity's most important systems for organizing value, trust, obligation, and cooperation.

Invitation to the Reader

If this book changed the way you think about money, don't stop with money.

Look at your time.

Look at your skills.

Look at your relationships.

Look at your assets.

Look at your promises.

Look at your business.

Ask:

What value do I possess?

Then ask the more important question:

How easily can I make that value useful to someone else?

That is where economics becomes personal.

Closing Thought

Before there was money, there was exchange.

Before there was exchange, there was need.

Before there were markets, there was trust.

And behind all of them was the same human question:

"How can what I have become what you need?"

That question created barter.

It encouraged credit.

It shaped money.

It built markets.

And it continues to shape the economic world we inhabit today.

www.ingramcontent.com/pod-product-compliance
Lightning Source LLC
LaVergne TN
LVHW050807061126
851857LV00012B/712